D0205265

DATE DUE

THE VIEW FROM THE TOWER

Theodore Ziolkowski

The View from
the Tower

ORIGINS OF AN
ANTIMODERNIST
IMAGE

PRINCETON UNIVERSITY PRESS
PRINCETON, N. J.

Copyright © 1998 by Princeton University Press
Published by Princeton University Press, 41 William Street,
Princeton, New Jersey 08540
In the United Kingdom: Princeton University Press,
Chichester, West Sussex

Library of Congress Cataloging-in-Publication Data
Ziolkowski, Theodore.
The view from the tower : origins of an antimodernist
image / Theodore Ziolkowski.
p. cm.
Includes bibliographical references and index.
ISBN 0–691–05907–1 (alk. paper)
1. Modernism (Literature) 2. Literature, Modern—
History and criticism. 3. Literary landmarks.
4. Towers. I. Title.
PN56.M54Z56 1998
809'.933112—dc21   97-52100

This book has been composed in Garamond and Caslon
Designed by Jan Lilly
Composed by Eileen Reilly

Princeton University Press books are printed
on acid-free paper and meet the guidelines for
permanence and durability of the Committee on
Production Guidelines for Book Longevity
of the Council on Library Resources

http://pup.princeton.edu

Printed in the United States of America

10 9 8 7 6 5 4 3 2 1

FOR MY BROTHER

John Edmund Ziolkowski

CONTENTS

LIST OF ILLUSTRATIONS   ix

PREFACE   xi

ACKNOWLEDGMENTS   xvii

CHAPTER ONE
The Proud Towers   3

CHAPTER TWO
William Butler Yeats: The Tower of Visions   41

CHAPTER THREE
Robinson Jeffers: The Tower beyond Time   69

CHAPTER FOUR
Rainer Maria Rilke: The Tower of Desire   97

CHAPTER FIVE
Carl Gustav Jung: The Tower of the Psyche   131

CHAPTER SIX
The Broken Towers   149

NOTES   175

INDEX   191

ILLUSTRATIONS

1. Pieter Bruegel the Elder, *The Tower of Babel*   4

2. Babylon of Nebuchadnezzar II   9

3. Saint Barbara with Tower   16

4. Campanile of Sant'Apollinare in Classe, Ravenna   18

5. Bamberg Cathedral   20

6. Chartres Cathedral   20

7. Minster of Our Gracious Lady, Ulm   21

8. Athanasius Kircher, *Turris Babel*   22

9. Hermann Hugo, *Pia Desideria*   24

10. Samuel Palmer, *The Lonely Tower*   24

11. Ivory-tower reliquary   32

12. Thoor Ballylee   42

13. Hawk Tower   70

14. Hawk Tower and Tor House   76

15. Robinson Jeffers at Hawk Tower   92

16. Château de Muzot   98

17. Auguste Rodin, *La Tour du Travail*   104

18. Tower of St.-Niklaas, Veurne   107

19. Rainer Maria Rilke on the balcony at Muzot   120

20. The first tower at Bollingen   132

21. The tower-complex at Bollingen   140

22. Carl Gustav Jung at Bollingen   147

23. The Kaiser Wilhelm Memorial Church, Berlin   150

24. The tower at Sissinghurst Castle   166

25. Prayer tower at Oral Roberts University   173

This essay represents yet another episode in a project that has engaged my attention for a good many years: the turn to the past as a manifestation of cultural conservatism in Europe and the United States following World War I. While the general impulse is familiar to literary history under a variety of names—the Conservative Revolution, the Creative Restoration, the Third Humanism, or the New Humanism—I have been interested in more specific manifestations of the tendency. In *The Classical German Elegy, 1795–1950* (Princeton, NJ: Princeton University Press, 1980) I sought to demonstrate the persistence into the twentieth century of a traditional form, which in German literature observes strict conventions governing metrics, structure, and content. In *Virgil and the Moderns* (Princeton, NJ: Princeton University Press, 1993) it was my aim to show how and why the figure of the Roman poet, as well as his works, were apprehended by a group of European and American writers of the twenties and thirties as images of continuity and value. In these books as well as various articles, whether they focus on figure, form, or work, the common denominator is the turn to tradition as a bulwark against what many writers and thinkers regarded as the anarchy loosed upon the world as a result of spiritual, intellectual, and political upheavals of the early twentieth century—as their response, in short, to the cultural despair of the age.

My interest in the present aspect of the larger subject emerged from an engagement with Rilke's poetry in my teaching and research. The topic first began to take shape when I read Jung's memoirs and realized that the poet and the psychologist were both at the same time living in towers just across the Swiss Alps from each other. As I began to explore more systematically the history and meaning of towers and their significance in the thought and works of Rilke and Jung, I came first to Yeats and then to Jeffers as other contemporaries who not only inhabited towers but in whose works towers constituted a central image for their resistance to many aspects of the modern world surrounding them. Once is an instance. Twice is a coincidence. But three times, for the student of comparative literature, becomes grounds for comparison.

While the title of this essay refers to the actual towers that the four writers sought out and to the fact that they all viewed their towers as retreats from which to contemplate the world, the subtitle focuses the topic in several important ways. In the first place, the four writers saw themselves as being outside, and often opposed to, the groups conventionally regarded as "modernist," if we take as our measure such Anglo-American poets as Pound, Eliot, and Stevens or novelists like Joyce, Woolf, and Lewis. Yeats is rarely (and Jeffers never!) included in studies dealing with "Makers of the New" or "the Pound Era." Rilke, who is not numbered among such arch-modernists as the German Expressionists, was specifically excluded by Gottfried Benn from the modernist canon of poetry stemming from Mallarmé. And Jung increasingly distanced himself from Freud and his followers by his turn to mythic archetypes. It should be self-evident that I do not share the often mindless denigration of Jeffers by the Marxist critics of the thirties and the New Critics of the forties; I am in sympathy, rather, with such recent poets as Gary Snyder, William Everson, James Tate (in his poem "Failed Tribute to the Stonemason of Tor House, Robinson Jeffers"), and Mark Jarman (in his poetic narrative *Iris*, 1992), who see in Jeffers the leading heir of an American tradition extending back to Whitman.

In the second place, the tower had more than spatial dimensions in the eyes of its inhabitants; it was also, even principally, an image with powerful associations. As a refuge it is specifically opposed by all four writers to the urban technological world of modernism to which they saw themselves in opposition. In contrast, as we shall have occasion to remark, the classic modernists often adduced the tower as a negative icon, as a symbol of the past that they hoped to overturn.

Finally, the subtitle indicates the historical and biographical approach of this work. Chapter 1 sketches the origins of the tower-image in cultural history and the associations that accrued to that image over the centuries. Chapters 2 through 5 survey the biographical circumstances that led the writers, from case to case, to their towers, and analyze the various manifestations of the image in their works. Chapter 6, in conclusion, traces the transformations of the image following its brief efflorescence in the 1920s.

This work began as a slide-lecture that I have had the opportunity and benefit of presenting to many audiences in Europe and the United States. Ten years ago I began to turn the lecture into an article, but it quickly became apparent that the material could not be adequately encompassed and persuasively explored within the scope of a normal journal piece. As I thought further about the topic, several valuable and handsomely illustrated works by architectural historians on the history of towers were published: notably the books (cited in the notes to chapter 1) by Van Leeuwen (1986), by Heinle and Leonhardt (1989), and by Minkowski (1991). Other matters intervened, and I did not take up the work seriously again until the winter of 1995–96. The result is the present jeu d'esprit, which I hope will interest other literary turriphiles.

Methodologically this essay belongs to the mode of literary study known as thematics, which has recently enjoyed a notable revival of interest in this country: for example, my own *Varieties of Literary Thematics* (Princeton, NJ: Princeton University Press, 1983); *The Return of Thematic Criticism*, ed. Werner Sollors (Cambridge: Harvard University Press, 1993); Horst S. and Ingrid G. Dämmrich, *Spirals and Circles: A Key to Thematic Patterns in Classicism and Realism* (New York: Lang, 1994); and *Thematics Reconsidered*, ed. Frank Trommler (Amsterdam: Rodopi, 1995). The aim of such studies is not simply to catalog occurrences but, rather, to identify the presence of a theme, motif, or image as symptomatic of a profound concern in the thought and work of an individual writer and, thereby, to link that writer's oeuvre meaningfully to that of others exhibiting similar patterns. In the present case the literary image assumes an unusual immediacy owing to the fact that the writers actually acquired or built towers as places of habitation: they actualized their resistance to modern society and its values by taking up residence in towers that embodied the past and its cultural associations. It is my endeavor in this essay to point out the similarities linking Yeats, Jeffers, Rilke, and Jung in their common obsession with towers and, at the same time, to underscore the characteristic differences that distinguish their various turriphilias. The ultimate goal is of course to achieve a deeper understanding and appreciation of their works. (All translations, unless otherwise indicated, are my own.)

As usual, my work has benefited from the generous assistance of many people. Mary Murrell of Princeton University Press expressed a gratifying interest in the topic long before the book was completed. Thanks to her, the manuscript received authoritative readings by two scholars whose work I greatly admire: Edward Engelberg, who in *The Vast Design: Patterns in W. B. Yeats's Aesthetics* (2d ed. 1988) has made the most persuasive case for Yeats's modernism; and Werner Sollors, a splendid comparatist and one of the prime movers of thematic studies. Once again, I am grateful to Lauren Lepow for her fine editorial hand and to Jan Lilly for her perceptive designer's eye. Writers who have had to find, and obtain permission for, illustrations for their works know how dependent we are on the kindness of strangers. My debts in this connection are mentioned in the acknowledgments; but here I would like to single out Deborah Tegarden and Jamie Orr at Princeton University Press for their special assistance. My friend William McGuire, a knowledgeable Jungian, alerted me to the biography of Christiana Morgan by Claire Douglas, which is mentioned in the last chapter. My three children—Margaret, Jan, and Eric Ziolkowski—have made from their own fields valuable suggestions that they will recognize in the text. Eric and my son-in-law Robert Thurston made separate trips to Ireland in July and August 1997 and brought back from Yeats's Thoor Ballylee several excellent photographs that confronted me with a grateful *embarras du choix*. And my wife Yetta not only helped me to identify the most appropriate images for the book; she also spent an hour circling the Kaiser Wilhelm Memorial Church in Berlin to capture the most revealing view of that striking monument.

Theodore Ziolkowski
Princeton, New Jersey
1 September 1997

ACKNOWLEDGMENTS

For their assistance in obtaining the illustrations for this volume I would like to express my appreciation to the following individuals and institutions: Karen Richter, Barbara Ross, and Betsy Rosasco of The Art Museum, Princeton University; William L. Joyce, Charles E. Greene, Margaret Sherry, and the staff of the Department of Rare Books and Special Collections, Firestone Library, Princeton University; Robert P. Matthews of the Office of Communications and Publications, Princeton University; Liliane Opsomer of the Belgian Tourist Office, New York, and the staff of the Dienst voor Toerisme, Veurne; Jesse Pisors, Assistant Director for Public Relations, Oral Roberts University, Tulsa, Oklahoma; Anna-Maria Schühlein of Tourismus & Kongreß Service, Bamberg; Jacques Vilain and Daniel Arcangeli of the Musée Rodin, Paris; Adriane von Hoop of Insel Verlag, Frankfurt am Main; Paul Spruhan of The Oriental Institute Museum, Chicago; Edouard Fiévet of Photo Fiévet, Chartres; Ina Bernath of Tourismuszentrale Ulm; Dr. Theo Jülich of the Hessisches Landesmuseum Darmstadt; Dr. John Hicks of the Robinson Jeffers Tor House Foundation, Carmel; Camilla Costello of Country Life Picture Library, London; Alexandrea Mikulczik of the Kunsthistorisches Museum, Vienna; and Mary K. Hartley of the Italian Goverment Tourist Board, New York.

THE VIEW FROM THE TOWER

The Proud Towers

Fig. 1. Pieter Bruegel the Elder, *The Tower of Babel* (1563). Permission of Kunsthistorisches Museum, Vienna.

□ 1 □

The vogue of tower habitation in the years immediately following World War I surely constitutes one of the more remarkable phenomena in the history of poetic ecology. Like Simeon the Stylite and his ascetic followers, who sought refuge from the temptations of late antiquity atop their pillars in the desert, these modern "turrites" took to their towers as strongholds of security in what they regarded as the wasteland of Western civilization. In 1919 William Butler Yeats and his family spent the first of several summers in Thoor Ballylee, a Norman castle twenty miles inland from the Atlantic coast of Ireland. The following year, on a bluff overlooking the Pacific near Carmel, Robinson Jeffers laid the first stones of Hawk Tower, where he was to live and write for the next forty years. In 1921 Rainer Maria Rilke moved into the Château de Muzot, the step-gabled thirteenth-century tower in the Swiss canton of Valais where he passed the remaining five years of his life. In 1923 Carl Gustav Jung built the squat tower on the upper Lake of Zurich that became the cornerstone of his compound at Bollingen and for four decades his private sanctuary of introspection.

Other artists and thinkers of the twentieth century also fancied towers. When Gerhart Hauptmann commissioned his villa in 1901 at Wiesenstein near Agnetendorf, he specified a corner tower, with a view of the Silesian forests, to which he liked to withdraw for meditation. But towers play no conspicuous role in his writings, and in any case he always went downstairs to the library to dictate his texts. Paul Hindemith lived from 1923 to 1927 in the "Cow-Herd's Tower" ("Kuhhirtenturm") on the city walls of Frankfurt-Sachsenhausen, but the opera and song cycle that he composed there offer no resonance of his abode. Similarly, off and on from 1927, when he became headmaster of the Beacon Hill School, until 1937, Bertrand Russell maintained his study in the tower of Telegraph House on the Sussex Downs—again with no discernible impact on his thought.

What distinguishes Yeats, Jeffers, Rilke, and Jung is the fact that they not only spent years living in towers; towers play a constitutive role, both literal and symbolic, in their writings. Whether these writers share any characteristics that might account for their common turriphilia, and whether by moving into towers they reified an image already prevalent in their works or, alternatively, by writing about towers internalized the reality of their lives—these are some of the questions to be addressed in the following pages.

◨ 2 ◨

Let us begin by asking precisely what we mean when we say "tower." The standard architectural definition—a structure whose height is disproportionate with reference to its base—does not get us very far. The towers inhabited by our four writers have spiritual dimensions rather than architectonic ones. In this respect they exemplify an ancient tradition. Joseph Campbell once suggested that "the most striking symbolic features of the earliest high culture centers of both the Old World and the New were the great temple towers and pyramids rising high above the humble rooftops clustered about their bases."[1] All these towers—from the storied pagodas of the Far East and the stupas of Southeast Asia to the obelisks of Egypt and the great stepped temples of Central America—occupy a similar place in their respective cultures: they represent the cosmic mountain regarded as the home of deity and thus reunite symbolically a heaven and earth that were originally one.[2] Just as the ancient Hebrews imagined Jehovah on Mount Horeb in the Sinai, the Greeks located their gods on Mount Olympus; the Indians situated Siva's earthly retreat on the mythic Mount Meru at the center of the world; Hindus, Buddhists, and Muslims alike venerated Adam's Peak in Sri Lanka; the Japanese regarded Mount Fuji as the habitation of the supreme Shinto deity; and Buddhist temples in Korea still feature a small shrine to the indigenous mountain god.

To the extent that upward-striving towers exemplify the human desire to transcend the restraints of temporal existence and restore the contact between heaven and earth that was shattered by the Fall, they differ profoundly in their religious function from the great pyramids of Egypt, whose stereometric mass invites our attention not upward but inward, where they enclose bodies and treasures.[3] (Pyramids evolved in the fifth millennium B.C. from the dwarf walls that originally surrounded the sunken burial chambers of the inhabitants of the Nile Valley.) In its original religious capacity, therefore, the tower stands alone as the embodiment of pure vertical structure: its space neither contains nor functions. Fortress towers, which are not independent structures, came later, as did such functional forms as lighthouses, bell towers, watchtowers, guard towers, water towers, radio towers, and other modern adaptations.

◧ 3 ◨

Of the various towers that punctuated the landscape of the ancient world the oldest and, for Western civilization, most influential were the terrace temples of Mesopotamia. The great stepped tower that the Hebrews saw in Babylon when Nebuchadnezzar brought them there in 587 B.C. marked the high point of a tradition reaching back three or four thousand years. Why the early inhabitants of the Mesopotamian basin began building their temples on terraced elevations is still a matter of debate. According to one theory the Sumerians migrated to the plains of southern Mesopotamia from a mountainous land where they had been accustomed to worship their deities on heights; the terrace temples represented their effort to reproduce by artificial means the elevations that their spirituality required.[4] Another view, taking the climatic conditions of southern Mesopotamia into account, proposes that frequent floods necessitated locating the temples on earthen elevations which, as they were repaired and improved, grew higher and higher. In any case, excavations have shown that the earliest strata go back to the fifth millennium.[5] In the course of the fourth millennium, great terrace temples were erected in Eridu, Uruk, Nippur, Ur, and other centers of southern Mesopotamia—centuries before Babylon became a city of any importance.

Fig. 2. Babylon of Nebuchadnezzar II (oil painting by
Maurice Bardin, after a watercolor by Herbert Anger,
based on suggestions by Prof. Eckhart Unger). Courtesy
of the Oriental Institute of the University of Chicago.

At the peak of Sumerian civilization it was the function
of these towering ziggurats to symbolize, as Campbell
puts it, "the graded stages of a universal manifestation of
divinity."[6] As the worshiper climbed past the seven
stepped terraces, he not only moved through the levels
between earth and heaven as represented by the seven
planetary deities but also advanced through the seven
grades of human consciousness, until he reached the

sanctuary containing the inner shrine that constituted the seat of whichever supreme deity was worshiped locally. At the same time, these spatiotemporal models of heavenly and earthly life also provided excellent observation posts for the priests, whose astronomical investigations caused the ziggurats, especially in the course of the first millennium B.C., to acquire a reputation as places of intellectual activity.

If the tower originally possessed an essentially religious or spiritual meaning and provided the locus for the encounter of god and mortals, the rituals symbolizing the reunification of heaven and earth had implications that led to two other important associations. According to Herodotus (1.181–82), who visited Babylon around 460 B.C., the spacious temple on the summit held a richly adorned couch of unusual size. "There is no statue of any kind set up in the place, nor is the chamber occupied of nights by any one but a single native woman, who, as the Chaldaeans, the priests of this god, affirm, is chosen for himself by the deity out of all the women of the land." Herodotus also reports, though he disclaims any belief in the story, that the god reputedly comes down in person and sleeps upon the couch with the priestess—a legend that probably goes back to an early stage when the ruler and the priestess reenacted ritually the symbolic reunification of heaven and earth. Good comparatist that he is, Herodotus relates this account to stories about the priestesses of the temple of Theban Zeus in Egypt and the temple of Apollo at Patara. In all these cases the woman is prohibited from intercourse with mortal men. We note, therefore, that the tower, initially a religious site, soon acquired connotations of sexuality as well as sequestration—connotations that have persisted down to the psychoanalytical theories of Freud and his followers. The origins of Etemenanki, the great tower of Babylon located next to the ancient sanctuary of Marduk, are still obscure. According to prevailing opinion, construction of this largest of the Mesopotamian ziggurats may well have been undertaken during the reign of Nebuchadnezzar I (1123–1101 B.C.), who defeated the Elamites and recovered the great statue of Marduk that had been taken away as booty earlier in the century.[7] In an effort to surpass all existing terrace temples, Nebuchadnezzar planned an edifice that rose to a height of ninety-one meters on a base of ninety-one by ninety-one meters. For five centuries, however, the massive structure remained uncompleted until Nebuchadnezzar II (605–562 B.C.) made it his great obligation to the god Marduk as well as his ancestors to complete Etemenanki.

The tower of Babylon was not identical with the Tower of Babel that entered Western consciousness through the text of the Old Testament. Chapter 11 of Genesis was written by the scribe known as J sometime in the tenth century B.C.—several hundred years before his descendants in the Babylonian Captivity toiled at the completion of Nebuchadnezzar's great project. Whether he was inspired by the sight of actual ziggurats and ruins or knew them only from literary tradition is not certain. In either case, the Hebrews of the tenth century would have been dumbfounded by the massive towers of Mesopotamia. Although the notion of the encounter with deity on great heights was not unknown to them—witness the story of Moses' ascent of Mount Horeb to receive the Tables of Law—the idea of erecting artificial mountains for that purpose was totally alien to them.

11

Moreover, the Bible often depicts mountain heights as places of evil or temptation. According to Ezekiel (20.28–31), who was contemptuous of the fertility cults associated with high places, God was angered because the early Hebrews offered their sacrifices on mountaintops and "presented the provocation of their offering." In the New Testament, too, Satan takes Jesus to lofty places—the pinnacle of the temple and a very high mountain—in order to tempt him (Matt. 4.5–9). Failing to appreciate the religious significance of the Babylonian edifices, the Hebrews saw in them a manifestation of human arrogance—a view that might have been reinforced by the intellectual pretensions of the Babylonian astronomers. Certainly the Hebrews could only have been offended by the notion of a god who lowered himself to couple with an earthly priestess.

Accordingly, the exalted Sumerian view of the tower as an image for the ascent of consciousness and the locus for the encounter with the divine was completely inverted by the Hebrews, in whose moralistic imagination the ruined or uncompleted ziggurats suggested not the humble approach to one's god but an act of titanic arrogance punished by the god with destruction. "Come, let us build ourselves a city, and a tower with its top in the heavens, and let us make a name for ourselves, lest we be scattered abroad upon the face of the whole earth" (Gen. 11.4).

The appeal of this notion to the Hebrew mind is attested by the fact that this story, unlike many other legends in Genesis, such as the Garden of Paradise or the Flood, has no parallel in Babylonian myth and shows many signs of having been originally composed by a non-Babylonian writer.[8] That a ziggurat should have been destroyed by a Babylonian deity whose cozy sanctuary it provided is much less likely than that it should have been shattered by the wrathful Jehovah of the early Hebrews. Most Babylonian texts evince pride in the building of cities and towers. The use of brick and bitumen as building materials would have seemed unusual only to an observer accustomed, like the residents of Palestine, to stone as the basic unit of construction. Finally, the biblical etymology—"Therefore is the name of it called Babel; because the LORD did there confound the language of all the earth . . ." (Gen. 11:9)—makes sense only for a speaker who does not understand the Sumerian meaning of the name ("gate of god") and derives it instead from Hebrew *balal* ("to confuse"). In short, the legend was presumably invented by Hebrews emerging from the simplicity of nomadic existence as an account of the fragmentation of primitive unity into separate communities, as their response to the technological achievements of the more advanced Babylonian civilization, and as an indictment of human *superbia* vis-à-vis the divine.[9]

▣ 4 ▣

By the time of the Babylonian Captivity and Herodotus's visit to Babylon, the tower—specifically in the form of the ziggurat—had accumulated several distinct associations that were to play a significant role in its cultural apprehension. Foremost among these was the tower as a place of religious or spiritual experience, to which was attached a secondary association of intellectual insight. Where the Hebrew mind saw the haughty aspiration to power, the Greek imagination detected evidences of sexuality. For centuries, however, these associations lay as dormant as the ruins of the Mesopotomian ziggurats themselves.

It is one of the oddities of architectural history that the tower, after having occupied such a prominent place during several millennia of Sumerian history, played virtually no role in classical antiquity.[10] The Greeks, in accordance with their general aesthetic principles, rejected for their own purposes any structure as asymmetrical as the tower.[11] Even in the Alexandrine period the great lighthouse of Alexandria, the Pharos, was regarded as such an idiosyncrasy that it was numbered among the seven wonders of the ancient world.[12] While the Romans had towers, they lacked any appreciation for the freestanding, functionless tower and built only structures that had a practical purpose, such as lighthouses or watchtowers on fortresses. (These may have been modeled in part on the Minoan *nuraghi*, squat round defensive towers from the second millennium B.C. that they could see in Corsica, Sicily, and Southern Italy—but especially in Sardinia.[13] These primordial towers, often erected on ancestral graves, also embodied a magical link to the dead.)[14]

In their literature and folklore, however, both Greeks and Romans were acquainted with certain symbolic aspects of the tower. While Lucretius does not specify a tower, in *De rerum natura* he created an unforgettable image of the serene temples from which the wise may look down upon the tribulations of the world:

> sed nil dulcius est bene quam munita tenere
> edita doctrina sapientum templa serena,
> despicere unde queas alios passimque videre
> errare atque viam palantis quaerere vitae. . . .
>
> (2.7–10)

Fig. 3. Antoine Bourdell, *Sainte Barbe*
(1916). Courtesy of The Art Museum,
Princeton University. Gift of the
J. Lionberger Davis, Class of 1900,
Art Trust.

evident in the early Christian legend of Saint Barbara.
The daughter of a heathen who kept her confined in a
tower with two windows, she had a third window added
to complete the Trinity and, for her Christian faith, suffered the resulting martyrdom. She is represented icono-
graphically as holding, or standing in front of, a tower
with three windows.

provided is much less likely than that it should have been shattered by the wrathful Jehovah of the early Hebrews. Most Babylonian texts evince pride in the building of cities and towers. The use of brick and bitumen as building materials would have seemed unusual only to an observer accustomed, like the residents of Palestine, to stone as the basic unit of construction. Finally, the biblical etymology—"Therefore is the name of it called Babel; because the LORD did there confound the language of all the earth . . ." (Gen. 11:9)—makes sense only for a speaker who does not understand the Sumerian meaning of the name ("gate of god") and derives it instead from Hebrew *balal* ("to confuse"). In short, the legend was presumably invented by Hebrews emerging from the simplicity of nomadic existence as an account of the fragmentation of primitive unity into separate communities, as their response to the technological achievements of the more advanced Babylonian civilization, and as an indictment of human *superbia* vis-à-vis the divine.[9]

◻ 4 ◻

By the time of the Babylonian Captivity and Herodotus's visit to Babylon, the tower—specifically in the form of the ziggurat—had accumulated several distinct associations that were to play a significant role in its cultural apprehension. Foremost among these was the tower as a place of religious or spiritual experience, to which was attached a secondary association of intellectual insight. Where the Hebrew mind saw the haughty aspiration to power, the Greek imagination detected evidences of sexuality. For centuries, however, these associations lay as

◙ 5 ◙

Towers in their recognizably "modern" form are a product of the Christian Middle Ages as part of ecclesiastical architecture—initially in the form of such early freestanding towers as the campaniles of Ravenna or the Irish round towers or *turres ecclesiasticae*. (A development analogous to the freestanding bell towers in the West can be seen in the minarets of Islamic mosques, which dominate the landscape from the Taj Mahal in India to the Mosque of Mopti in West Africa.)[15] Subsequently attached to churches and cathedrals, they made their appearance from the eighth to the thirteenth century, often in multiples. The four towers that were a popular adornment on larger Romanesque churches were often related symbolically to the four gospels[16] or exemplified the aggressive spirit of a church militant.[17] Originally these ecclesiastical towers had the same religious function as the ancient ziggurats—to direct the viewer's attention to the heavens. But gradually the religious superstructures also took on associations of power, if not *superbia*, as cathedrals— for instance, those of Cologne, Munich, Regensburg, Chartres, Paris—came to be identified as the seat of episcopal authority by the twin towers rising above the west facade. (The Cistercian order included in their rules a "tower prohibition" in order to avoid any hint of worldly power in their architecture.) By way of contrast, churches built by towns—for example, those of Ulm and Freiburg, and St. Stefan's in Vienna—were identified by a single spire. This principle was carried through so consistently that the great edifice at Strasbourg, which was begun as

Fig. 4. Campanile of Sant'Apollinare in
Classe, Ravenna. Photograph by Foto-ENIT-
Roma. Courtesy of the Italian Government
Tourist Board, New York.

an episcopal cathedral with twin towers, eventually was
completed with only a single spire after the citizens of the
town took it over.[18]

In the centuries before town halls were built, most
important civil legal actions—notably court hearings,
marriages, town meetings—took place in the porch of
the west facade beneath the tower that was regarded as
symbolic of civic authority.[19] As the town halls of the
Renaissance began to be built, the single tower was

adapted to its architecture, especially in northern Europe. (The Italian aversion toward the Gothic resulted in the almost total absence of towers on churches and palaces during the Renaissance[20]—despite the presence in the thirteenth and fourteenth centuries of the so-called Tribal Towers, which still dominate the skyline of such towns as San Gimignano, "the city of beautiful towers.") The new popularity of "civic towers" in architecture north of the Alps was paralleled by a conspicuous revival of interest in the biblical Tower of Babel. During the sixteenth century that image provided one of the most frequent subjects in northern European art, from an early woodcut of Hans Holbein the Elder (1526) by way of Pieter Bruegel the Elder and Paul Bril down to Maerten van Valckenborch's masterpiece of 1595.[21] Stimulated by this interest, the great encyclopedists of the seventeenth century brought all their learning to bear on the topic in such vast compendia as Athanasius Kircher's *Turris Babel* (Amsterdam, 1679).

Paradoxically, just as the artists and thinkers of the Reformation began to emphasize in the tower the biblical attributes of pride and power, others were recovering its original reputation as a place of intellect and spiritual introspection. For instance, in a sixteenth-century engraving depicting the "Allégorie de la Grammaire" the various aspects of language are shown as a tower extending from a foundation provided by the alphabet to the lofty twin ramparts of prosody and syntax.[22] It was in his tower in Wittenberg that Martin Luther, in 1513, underwent what German theologians call his *Turmerlebnis* ("tower experience")—the insight that the true path to salvation leads through faith, as expressed in Rom. 1.16–

Fig. 5 (top left). Bamberg Cathedral. Courtesy of
Tourismus & Kongreß Service, Bamberg.

Fig. 6 (bottom left). Chartres Cathedral. Permission
of Photo Fiévet, Chartres.

Fig. 7 (above). Minster of Our Gracious Lady, Ulm.
Courtesy of Stadtarchiv Ulm and Tourismuszentrale Ulm.

Fig. 8. Frontispiece from Athanasius Kircher, *Turris Babel* (1679). Courtesy of Department of Rare Books and Special Collections. Princeton University Library.

17: "For it is the power of God unto salvation to every one that believeth." A few decades later (1588) it was in the tower described so affectionately in his essays that Montaigne meditated. His study, he tells us, is a perfectly round room on the third floor of a tower from which he can overlook the gardens and almost all sections of his house. When he is in that library, he is fully in his own kingdom of the mind. "C'est là mon siège." He seeks there to surrender himself to "la domination pure" and to remove this corner from all community—conjugal, filial, and civil alike.[23] And in the introduction to *The Anatomy of Melancholy* (1621), Robert Burton tells his reader: "I am not poor, I am not rich; *nihil est, nihil deest,* I have little, I want nothing: all my treasure is in *Minerva's* tower."[24]

If the tower showed up in medieval iconography as an image of human pride, suggested by the figure of a man plunging headlong from its heights,[25] the emblem books of the seventeenth century depicted a tower illuminated at its summit as the symbol of the guiding spiritual light.[26] For instance, in Hermann Hugo's *Pia Desideria* (1628) the faithful pilgrim is directed across the labyrinth of life by an angel with flaming torch atop a distant tower, to illustrate the words from Ps. 119.5: "O that my ways were directed to keep thy statutes." Milton's conjuration in "Il Penseroso" of the solitary thinker sitting in his tower by lamplight and perusing mystical or Neoplatonic doctrines is representative of this view:

> Or let my lamp at midnight hour
> Be seen in some high lonely tower,
> Where I may oft outwatch the Bear,
> With thrice great Hermes, or unsphere
> The spirit of Plato to unfold
> What worlds or what vast regions hold
> The immortal mind that hath forsook
> Her mansions in this fleshly nook; . . .

> (Lines 85–92)

As familiarized by Samuel Palmer's etching *The Lonely Tower* (1879) it provided an unforgettable image seized upon by Milton's successors in the twentieth century.

Fig. 9. From Hermann
Hugo, *Pia Desideria* (1628).
Courtesy of Department
of Rare Books and Special
Collections. Princeton
University Library.

Fig. 10. Samuel Palmer, *The Lonely Tower* (1879). Courtesy of
The Art Museum, Princeton University. Gift of Frank Jewett Mather, Jr.,
in 1947.

⊡ 6 ⊡

The tower as an image of contemplation was maintained during the sixteenth and seventeenth centuries by thinkers both religious and secular, but it entered the popular consciousness in the later eighteenth century along with the Gothic revival. While Horace Walpole was constructing his turreted castle at Strawberry Hill and William Beckford was erecting his "abbey" at Fonthill (which eventually collapsed under the weight of its tower!), Edmund Burke summoned up the tower as an image of the sublime, arguing that "a perpendicular has more force in forming the sublime, than an inclined plane. . . ."[27] As the tower became an essential element in the literary architecture of the Gothic romances of Mrs. Radcliffe as well as Beckford's *Vathek*,[28] the mystical associations remained central. Goethe's *Wilhelm Meister's Years of Apprenticeship* (*Wilhelm Meisters Lehrjahre*, 1795–96) displays the motifs common to the Gothic romance: the vaguely Masonic group that guides the hero's destiny, until his initiation into their number, is known as the Society of the Tower (*Gesellschaft vom Turm*) and holds its assemblies in a tower attached to Lothario's country house.

The age of romanticism knew all extremes of the symbolism of the tower, from spirituality to sexuality. In Shelley's poetry the tower beside a lake or stream often suggests quite generally a contrast between permanence and change.[29] But his towers, especially in the early works, also exploit the ancient associations of spiritual learning, as in the "tower of stone" in *The Revolt of Islam* (1818) within whose walls the hermit kept "many a tome

/ Whose lore had made that sage all that he had become"
(canto 4, strophes 1–3). The Miltonic association of tower, lamp, and Plato occurs in *Prince Athanase* (1817) to
describe the lofty room where the prince and his teacher
Zonoraas pore over the philosopher's "words of light":

> The Balearic fisher, driven from shore,
> Hanging upon the peakèd wave afar,
> Then saw their lamp from Laian's turret gleam,
> Piercing the stormy darkness, like a star. . . .
>
> (187–90)

The same prince is characterized metaphorically as one
whose

> soul had wedded Wisdom, and her dower
> Is love and justice, clothed in which he sate
> Apart from men, as in a lonely tower.　(31–33)

At the other extreme from Shelley and his youthful idealism, the young Alexandre Dumas *père* chose a tower on
the Seine as the symbol of sexual debauchery in his sensa-
tional historical drama *La Tour des Nesle* (1832): it was
here, according to Parisian legend, that the fourteenth-
century Queen Marguerite of Burgundy and her two
sisters-in-law entertained each night a new trio of hand-
some young men, whose corpses were invariably discovered the next morning floating in the water at the foot of
the tower.

While the Bastille and the Tower of London kept the
structure before the public eye as an image of imprison-
ment, such painters of German Romanticism as Caspar
David Friedrich, Karl Friedrich Schinkel, and Carl Gustav Carus featured the towers of cathedrals as symbols
of spirituality, and writers in every language invoked the

tower as an image of Lucretian serenity. In the second part of Goethe's *Faust* (1832) the watchman Lynkeus expresses the ambivalence of one who is privileged by his lofty position to see all but condemned by it to inactivity.

Zum Sehen geboren,
Zum Schauen bestellt,
Dem Turme geschworen,
Gefällt mir die Welt.   (11288–11291)

(Born to see, / Assigned to watch, / Sworn to the tower, / the world is my joy.)

Stendhal's *La Chartreuse de Parme* (1839) positively bristles with towers[30]—most spectacularly the Torre Farnese where Fabrice del Dongo is imprisoned for nine months as the result of a political intrigue. His prison cell—actually a wooden cage within a room in a turret built on the platform of another tower some 380 steps high—is the scene of Fabrice's love affair with Clélia and the center of action for much of the book. But the tower of equal interest in our context is the eighty-foot campanile in which the Abbé Blanès pursues his astrological observations. For it is here that the abbé—virtually a modern Chaldaean priest!—foretells Fabrice's future: that he will be imprisoned, will be tempted by crime, and will finally end his days like the abbé himself in a monastery, having renounced the luxury of the world. Sexuality, astrology, spirituality—all the Sumerian associations resound!

We find an odd inversion of the familiar Lucretian image in Annette von Droste-Hülshoff's well-known poem "At the Tower" ("Am Turme," 1841–42).[31] The writer introduces herself as a woman standing on the high

27

balcony of a tower with hair blowing maenadlike in stormy winds and circled by a shrieking starling (which will reappear at Yeats's tower):

> Ich steh auf hohem Balkone am Turm,
> Umstrichen vom schreienden Stare,
> Und laß gleich einer Mänade den Sturm
> Mir wühlen im flatternden Haare.

She longs to leap down and play in the waves below; to sit in a warship coursing like a seagull across the reefs; to be a hunter on the open field or a soldier. "If only I were a man!" ("Wär ich ein Mann doch mindestens nur"). But, like Danaë and Saint Barbara and Rapunzel before her, she is bound to her tower and can make no other gesture of freedom than to allow her hair to flutter in the breeze:

> Nun muß ich sitzen so fein und klar,
> Gleich einem artigen Kinde,
> Und darf nur heimlich lösen mein Haar
> Und lassen es flattern im Winde!

(Now I must sit so nice and proper, / like a well-mannered child, / and may do no more than loosen my hair stealthily / and let it flutter in the wind.)

Other writers were more taken with the image of pride. In "The City in the Sea" (1831; 1845), a poem based on the legend that the city of Gomorrah was sunk in punishment for its sins beneath the waters of the Dead Sea,[32] Edgar Allan Poe resurrected the tower in this ancient capacity.

> Lo! Death has reared himself a throne
> In a strange city lying alone

Far down within the dim West,
Where the good and the bad and the worst and
    the best
Have gone to their eternal rest.
There shrines and palaces and towers
(Time-eaten towers that tremble not!)
Resemble nothing that is ours.

In a striking image Poe describes the city submerged for
its arrogance (and, implicitly, its sexual license) beneath
the melancholy waters,

While from a proud tower in the town
Death looks gigantically down.

A decade later, in "The Bell-Tower" (in *The Piazza Tales*,
1856), Herman Melville adduced the same association-
laden image to epitomize the pride of an Italian Renaissance city-state and the arrogance of its mechanician, the
unblest foundling Bannadonna. "Enriched through commerce with the Levant, the state in which he lived voted
to have the noblest Bell-Tower in Italy. . . . Stone by
stone, month by month, the tower rose. Higher, higher,
snaillike in pace, but torch or rocket in its pride."[33] Built
like the Tower of Babel, "following the second deluge,
when the waters of the Dark Ages had dried up," Bannadonna's tower suffers the same fate; the mechanical bell-
mechanism kills its creator while the weight of the bell
implodes the belfry; and on the first anniversary of its
completion the whole tower collapses. "And so pride
went before the fall," the author concludes.

It remains to mention one further association that accrued to the tower during the romantic decades—the notion of the "ivory tower" that has been attached as a term

of opprobrium to the retreats of artists, scholars, and intellectuals ever since Sainte-Beuve famously applied it to his friend Alfred de Vigny.[34] The fact that Vigny's existence in the twin-towered manor of Maine-Giraud, in which he spent the last thirty years of his life (and cultivated the finest cognac in the Charente), was anything but a withdrawal is beside the point here.[35] For reality has been displaced by literature—that is, by the two lines in the poetic epistle "A M. Villemain" published in Sainte-Beuve's *Pensées d'août* (1837) in which, following a characterization of Lamartine and Hugo, it is remarked: ". . . et Vigny, plus secret, / Comme en sa tour d'ivoire, avant midi, rentrait."[36]

Erwin Panofsky assumed, and it was long accepted, that Sainte-Beuve's fateful phrase stemmed from a conflation of the bronze tower in Horace's account of Danaë and the famous passage in the Song of Songs (7.4) in which the bridegroom assures his bride that her neck is "as a tower of ivory": *collum tuum sicut turris eburnea.*[37] However, recent studies have shown that a continuous tradition of Old Testament exegesis and the popular cult associated with the Lauretian litany, along with numerous works of ecclesiastical art, bore the image from late antiquity down to the nineteenth century.[38] Early ecclesiological exegetes interpreted *turris eburnea* as the Church itself or as the learned father through whose teachings the devout learn the message of Christ (cf. the four towers of the evangelists that adorned the Romanesque churches). In these interpretations the "ivory tower" is read not as a metaphor for the neck of the beloved but, quite literally, as the building of the church itself. This reading, which was continuous in European theological thought down to the late eighteenth century, was paralleled by another important tradition, the Lauretian litany, in which Maria herself is envisaged in a multitude of hypostases, including an ivory tower:

> Rosa mystica, ora pro nobis.
> Turris Davidica, ora.
> Turris eburnea, ora.
> Domus aurea, ora.
> Foederis arca, ora.[39]

(Mystic rose, pray for us. / Tower of David, pray. /Ivory tower, pray. / Golden Domicile, pray. / Ark of the covenant, pray.)

The widespread popularity of this cult from the sixteenth century on expressed itself in ecclesiastical symbols, devotional pictures, church songs, and otherwise. Alongside the two literary traditions, finally, we can trace the image in the history of art, where small towers carved of ivory constitute an important part of liturgical equipment— for example, as containers for the sacraments, ciboria, chalices, and reliquaries. In any case, by the time Sainte-Beuve appropriated the phrase to designate Vigny's provincial retreat, the ivory tower was familiar in Christian literature and art as an image for refuge and a place of peaceful asylum.

◙ 7 ◙

By the second half of the nineteenth century the tower had become laden with so many symbolic associations that Browning could appropriately employ it as an open image devoid of specific meaning. In "Childe Roland to the Dark Tower Came" the "round squat turret, blind as

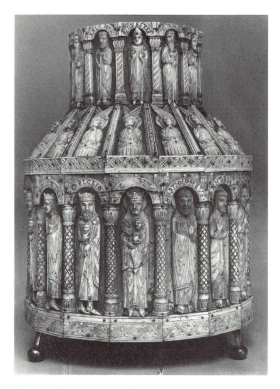

Fig. 11. Ivory-tower reliquary, early thirteenth century. Permission of Hessisches Landesmuseum Darmstadt.

the fool's heart, / Built of brown stone" (182–83)[40] is the obsessive goal of the narrator-hero's quest. But because the poem ends with the moment of his arrival at the Dark Tower and with no hint of its secret or his own future, it has been left to the critics to fill that mysterious space with their own hermeneutical ingenuities.

Other writers felt free to pick and choose among the available meanings for the image that for the fin de siècle became increasingly obsessive. Nietzsche was fond of heights—in his life, which often found him in his Alpine retreat in Sils Maria, and symbolically in his works. Already as a fourteen-year-old schoolboy at Schulpforta (in the fall of 1858) he made use of the Lucretian image in a poem describing an expedition with his classmates to the ruins of the nearby Schönburg. When they had climbed up to the castle, his companions rushed off to the *Keller* to sample the wine; but the youthful philosopher kept on climbing until he reached the lofty tower and looked around in wonder. While his classmates empty the kegs and pay homage to Bacchus, they leave him to what he calls, in a remarkably analogy to Montaigne's "domination pure," his *Herrscheramt* ("sovereign charge") on the tower:

Sie mögen dort in den Hallen
Nur zechen bis sie umfallen.
Ich übe mein Herrscheramt.[41]

(Let them carouse in the halls / until they collapse. / I shall exercise my sovereign charge.)

In 1879, moreover, having resigned his professorship at Basel, Nietzsche actually signed a six-year lease for a tower on the town wall near his mother's house in Naumburg, where he planned to raise fruits and vegetables in the moat and to reify his dream of tower-rule; but after only a few weeks his persistent headaches forced him to give up the idea, and he set out instead on the peregrinations that characterized his life for the next ten years.

In *Two on a Tower* (1882) Thomas Hardy exploited the traditional Sumerian associations of pride, sexuality, and astronomy: an eighteenth-century memorial tower, known as the Rings-Hill Speer, is the site where Swithin St. Cleeve, motivated by raw ambition, conducts his astronomical investigations and falls in love—or, at least, in passion—with Viviette Constantine, the wife of the property owner.

In the year that Gustave Eiffel thrust his great phallic tower into the heavens for the exposition in Paris, thereby creating one of the most compelling images for the hauteur of a world edging into modernity, Maurice Maeterlinck published his philosophical dramatic fairy tale *La Princesse Maleine* (1889), which is dominated by the windowless tower in which the princess is imprisoned by her parents when she refuses to renounce her claim of marriage on Prince Hjalmar. Ever since Danaë and Saint Barbara the tower has been the traditional site of sequestration for recalcitrant maidens. But Maleine, refusing to remain in this refuge, whose security is matched by its airless hermeticity, escapes into an earthly reality where she meets a very earthly end: she is strangled to death by her enemies.

A similar pattern is evident in Villiers de l'Isle-Adam's symbolist classic, *Axël* (1890), although the tower here represents spirituality rather than sequestration.[42] In act 3, which bears the heading "Le Monde Occulte," Maître Janus comes down from the tower where he has initiated Axël into the Kabbala, Hermetic lore, and Rosicrucian mysteries. This spokesman of a law transcending eternity ("le Loi suréternelle," 198) and of a spirit of universality uniting all being ("l'esprit d'universalité entre les choses," 196) seeks to persuade his pupil to renounce the world of substantial being. "Spiritualize your body; sublimate yourself" ("Spiritualise ton corps: sublime-toi"), he tells Axël (194); "The universe is nothing but a pretext for the development of total consciousness" (199). But Axël rejects his appeal and descends into the crypt of his castle in the Black Forest, where he meets his death. The protagonists of both these symbolist works, in short, turn away from the tower of spirituality and sequestration for the sake of life—albeit a life that brings them death. The turriphilia of the fin de siècle produced several characteristic oddities. In Denmark during the 1890s the leading symbolist journal was called *Tornet* (The tower). When V. I. Ivanov, the Berlin-educated classical philologist who became one of the leaders of the symbolist movement in Russia, established a Wednesday salon in St. Petersburg that became from 1905 to 1907 the meeting place for contemporary artists and authors, its location in his sixth-floor apartment, colored by associations from French Symbolism, led predictably to its designation as "The Tower."[43] Of course, any image that enjoys such widespread recognition will inevitably be parodied. The symbolist tower finds its parody in André Gide's *Paludes* (1895), which depicts a circle of aesthetic acquaintances so totally obsessed with themselves that they reject any intrusion of reality into their hermetic world. The narrator is writing a prose poem, entitled *Journal de Tityre ou Paludes*, about a man who lives alone in a tower surrounded by a vast swamp, where he fishes from the window with inadequate bait on a multiplicity of lines—a symbol (of symbolism itself!), as Gide reminds us: "insuffisance des amorces, multiplication des lignes (symbole)."[44] For Gide, who had earlier fled the Parisian literary scene for the bracing sensuality of North Africa, the tower clearly exemplifies the symbolist life he had rejected—the man so content with his own lot, as narrow as it may be, that he is unwilling to change or to set out on any journeys of self-discovery.[45]

In Ibsen's *The Master Builder* (1892) Solness also finds death, like Maleine and Axël, but his is no flight from a sheltering ivory tower. The soaring spire that lures him to his destruction is once again the proud tower of arrogance—a tower added idiosyncratically to a wholly secular house, perhaps in atonement for his earlier decision to stop building churches. And he is incited to his foolhardy act—climbing the scaffolding to place the wreath on the completed tower despite his severe acrophobia—not in order to encounter deity but for a symbolic sexual tryst. Only a few minutes earlier Hilda Wrangel had entranced him with her own vision of a castle standing on a height and thrusting up a tremendously high tower with a balcony on which she will stand, looking down with Lucretian haughtiness on ordinary mortals. It is her invitation to Solness to join her on that imaginary tower that prompts him to the daredevil feat that leads to his death.[46]

It was this citadel of nineteenth-century ideology that Barbara Tuchman had in mind when she appropriated from Poe's poem both the title and the motto for her "portrait of the world before the war, 1890–1914," *The Proud Tower* (1966). It is a phenomenon fatefully familiar from political history that powerful ideas and visions tend, in time, to be reified, and the same rule applies to science, where experiments test hypotheses. In 1910 the German architectural critic Joseph August Lux stated in the introduction to his *Ingenieur-Ästhetik* (Munich, 1910) that technology is nothing but the realization of ancient dreams: "At Babel a tower was built that men were not able to complete. Humanity has been dreaming ever since of the superhuman aspect of the Babylonian tower. But the technicians of today realized this dream and built skyscrapers, in comparison to which the highest towers of the earth appeared dwarflike."[47] If the cosmic mountain is the archetype of which the Tower of Babel provides the type, Thomas van Leeuwen suggests in his remarkable "metaphysics of the skyscraper," then every modern tower is a model that goes back ultimately to that Babylonian type.[48] Accordingly traditional images instantly sprang to the minds of European visitors to the United States when they saw the first skyscapers; they compared the skyline of New York City to that of San Gimignano or, repeatedly, to the Tower of Babel. American architects, in turn, looked to the stepped towers of the East or the cathedral towers of Europe as they sought inspiration for their lofty designs. Not surprisingly, the new skyscrapers became familiarly known as cathedrals, as in the "Cathedral of Commerce" (the Woolworth Building, 1913) or the "Cathedral of Learning" (University of Pittsburgh, 1926–37). Meanwhile, early-twentieth-century painters—Giorgio de Chirico, Delaunay, and Lyonel Feininger, among others—turned with growing fascination toward the tower or skyscaper as a representative subject for the modern world.

When Archibald MacLeish sailed for Europe in World War I, he left behind a volume of poems entitled *Tower of Ivory*.[49] While none of the poems refers specifically to towers, the volume as a whole reflects the neoromantic credo of the young Yale graduate who believed (in the poem "Realities") in the old transcendental verities:

> Yet when the splendor of the earth
>   Is fallen into dust,
> When plow and sword and fame and worth
>   Are rotted with black rust,

The Dream, still deathless, still unborn,
Blows in the hearts of men,
The star, the mystery, the morn
Bloom agelessly again.

As his friend Lawrence Mason observed in his foreword, the title "adequately represents his predominating idealistic conception, that against all the assaults of arid rationalism and crass materialism, against all the riddles of endless speculation and brutal experience, there is an impregnable tower of refuge into which man may enter, in the spirit, and find there the true values and eternal verities which alone can make him victorious over the world."

MacLeish's more ironic elder countryman, Henry James, was no longer able to find the tower of refuge so impregnable, although, in a novel left unfinished in August 1914, he made metaphorical use of the familiar image. The title of *The Ivory Tower* (1914) refers to an ivory cabinet fashioned in India after the model of a stepped tower and which serves as the receptacle for a letter transmitted to the hero, Graham Fielder, who has returned to America after many years abroad. But this precious objet d'art, even though it does not correspond to the by now traditional Western ivory tower of religion or symbolism, achieves symbolic status because it precisely epitomizes Graham's alienation from the corrupt life led by the wealthy New Yorkers depicted in the novel. "*Isn't* it an ivory tower," Gray says, when it is presented to him by his cousin Rosanna Gaw, "and doesn't living in an ivory tower just mean the most distinguished retirement?" Later a friend elaborates on this imagery:

"And it isn't so much too small . . . for you to get into it yourself, when you want to get rid of us, and draw the doors to. If it's a symbol of any retreat you really have an eye on I much congratulate you; I don't know what I wouldn't give myself for the 'run' of an ivory tower."[50]

He wonders ironically if Rosanna keeps "a choice assortment" of ivory towers and always has "a row of them ready for occupation." Indeed, he senses that it is "the formula of that young lady herself: perched aloft in an ivory tower is what *she* is." Henry James obviously thought so as well, for on the first page of the novel Rosanna is described as sheltered symbolically by a tower: "a vast pale-green parasol, a portable pavilion from which there fluttered fringes, frills and ribbons that made it resemble the roof of some Burmese palanquin or perhaps even pagoda." In fine, the governing image symbolizes the sheltered lives, the "proud tower" about to be destroyed by the events of the war. Because, with the outbreak of the war, James was no longer able to accept with equanimity the serenity and beauty of this life, the work remained a fragment.[51]

Our survey to this point has revealed a remarkable continuity in the various symbolic meanings associated with towers since classical antiquity—from spirituality and intellect by way of arrogance and sexuality to sequestration and refuge. We have also noted that several writers and thinkers along the way lived for a time in towers—Martin Luther, Montaigne, Vigny. However, the writers who lived in towers did not generally write about them. And those who wrote about them did not often live in towers and tended to appropriate the conventional associations of the image for the purpose of specific works. It remained for a few poets and thinkers *entre deux guerres* to bring life and art together in works about towers that were also written in parapeted and stepped towers surviving from the medieval past or sturdy new towers erected as bulwarks against decline and collapse. Yet within these retreats where they sought to preserve the past and from whose stability they could securely contemplate what their contemporary, Oswald Spengler, was diagnosing as the decline of Western civilization, each writer developed a characteristically personal image of the tower that marked his works.

CHAPTER TWO

William Butler Yeats:
The Tower of Visions

Fig. 12. Thoor Ballylee. Courtesy of Eric Ziolkowski.

In 1919, when William Butler Yeats (1865–1939) first occupied the Norman castle in County Galway that he
christened Thoor Ballylee, he was fifty-four years old and
entering a new phase of his life. The volume he published
that year, *The Wild Swans at Coole* (1919), comprises a
series of leave-takings. The book opens, following the
title-poem, with a pastoral elegy to Lady Gregory's son,
Yeats's young friend Robert Gregory, who had been shot
down over Italy as an airman in the war. Other poems
mourn the deaths of his relative Alfred Pollexfen and the
actress Mabel Beardsley. In a cycle of six poems Yeats lays
to rest his courtship of the beautiful Maud Gonne, who
in 1916 had for the last time and definitively rejected his
hand in marriage.

At least as traumatic for an Anglo-Irishman as the war
in Europe—because of conflicting loyalties, perhaps even
more so—was the Easter Rising of 1916,[1] and Yeats regis-
tered his dismay in a number of ballads published subsequently in the volume *Michael Robartes and the Dancer*
(1921): "Sixteen Dead Men" executed for their role in the
rebellion, "On a Political Prisoner" (his friend Con
Markievicz), and the four tragic heroes of "Easter 1916,"
from whose deaths "A terrible beauty is born" (180).[2] But
the Rising not only summoned forth heroism; it also
exposed profound flaws in the Irish national character.
"Romantic Ireland's dead and gone" (106), Yeats had
concluded several years earlier in the refrain to the poem

"September 1913." At that time he was dismayed by the cultural philistinism of the Irish middle classes, which had provoked riots at the opening of Synge's *The Playboy of the Western World* (1907) and initiated the controversy over Hugh Lane's bequest of his collection of French Impressionists to the Dublin National Gallery. By 1916, however, cultural disenchantment began to give way to radical social and political despair. "We have lost the ablest and most fine-natured of our young men," he wrote shortly after the rebellion. "A world seems to have been swept away."[3] The disaffected Celtic nationalist noted sadly how "The Leaders of the Crowd" exploited the Rising for their own political ends and "to keep their certainty accuse / All that are different of a base intent" (182). Even Countess Markievicz, the beautiful Constance Gore-Booth of his youth, "Blind and leader of the blind" (181), has been corrupted by the mob she sought to control. Losses and disillusionments of this kind came together to produce the apocalyptic vision of "The Second Coming" (1919), which begins with the falcon "turning in the widening gyre" as an image of social and political entropy—

> Things fall apart; the centre cannot hold;
> Mere anarchy is loosed upon the world . . .

> (184)

—and ends as that brutal symbol of the new age, the "rough beast" with blank and pitiless gaze, "Slouches toward Bethlehem to be born."

The year 1919, then, marked the beginning of a radical reassessment. The Easter Rising had exposed not just the naïveté of Yeats's youthful dreams of an Ireland united in Celtic mysticism and the untenability of his Fenian nationalism, but also the corruptibility of established law, custom, and morality. As he lamented bitterly in the ottava rima of the great stocktaking poem he wrote that year, "Nineteen Hundred and Nineteen":

> We too had many pretty toys when young:
> A law indifferent to blame or praise,
> To bribe or threat; habits that made old wrong
> Melt down, as it were wax in the sun's rays;
> Public opinion ripening for so long
> We thought it would outlive all future days.
> O what fine thought we had because we thought
> That the worst rogues and rascals had died out.
>
> (204)

Now, with the best of Anglo-Irish youth (and many Catholic Irish as well) killed off by the war in Europe, only rabble-rousers of the lower middle class that he despised are left. As Yeats put it in an open letter to Lady Gregory (1919), "Ireland has suffered more than England from democracy, for since the Wild Geese fled who might have grown to be leaders in manners and in taste, she has had but political leaders."[4] The oppressive measures undertaken during the Troubles in the name of the crown by the Black and Tans and the resistance of the Irish Republican Army triggered in Ireland widespread violence on both sides, which Yeats depicted in that same poem: "a drunken soldiery / Can leave the mother, murdered at her door, / To crawl in her own blood, and go scot-free" (205). Harsh realities exposed the futility of political idealism.

Yeats's move into Thoor Ballylee in 1919 amounted to a symbolic turn away from his own past dreams of Gaelic nationalism as well as a retreat before the reality of mob leadership and rebellion, a move from the modernism of the cities where he had spent much of his life—Dublin, London, Paris—to an ancient countryside that embodied the culture of Anglo-Irish gentry that was gradually coming to constitute his new ideal. And it marked the start of an altogether new mode of life with the wife he had married a year and a half earlier, Georgina (Georgie) Hyde-Lees, and their first child, who was was barely four months old.

◨ 2 ◨

Yeats first beheld the old square tower in 1896, when he made a walking tour in the west of Ireland with his friend Arthur Symons and was introduced to Lady Gregory at Coole Park.[5] Seeing it often thereafter on his frequent visits to Coole, he described the village of Ballylee with its castle and its legend of the beautiful Mary Hynes in 1899 in the essay "Dust Has Closed Helen's Eye."[6]

> I have lately been to a little group of houses, not many enough to be called a village, in the barony of Kiltartan in County Galway, whose name, Ballyless, is known through all the west of Ireland. There is the old square castle, Ballylee, inhabited by a farmer and his wife, and a cottage where their daughter and their son-in-law live, and a little mill with an old miller, and old ash-trees throwing green shadows upon a little river and great stepping stones.

In 1902, when the last tenant had died, the castle became part of the Gregory estate and then, in 1916, when the Congested Districts Board acquired part of the great estate for division into smaller parcels for purchase by individual landholders, was put up for sale.

In the winter of 1916–17 Yeats bought the tower from the Congested Districts Board for thirty-five pounds and renamed it Thoor Ballylee. As he explained, "Thoor is Irish for tower and it will keep people from suspecting us of modern gothic and a deer park. I think the harsh sound of 'Thoor' amends the softness of the rest."[7] In May of 1917, half a year before his marriage, he went to Ballylee to "take over my Tower."[8] "I shall make it habitable at no great expense and store there so many of my possessions that I shall be able to have less rooms in London. The Castle will be an economy, counting the capital I spend so much a year, and it is certainly a beautiful place." He planned initially to restore one of the cottages attached to the tower and then to undertake repairs to the tower itself. However, Yeats's early optimism was misplaced. It was no simple matter to restore the tower, which had fallen into such extensive disrepair—even the floors of the rooms were gone, along with most of the slate roof—that nobody else wanted it. The restoration of the cottage consumed much of the summer and fall of 1917—not to mention the honoraria for the lectures he delivered in Paris.[9] Yeats commissioned William A. Scott, "the drunken man of genius"[10] and professor of architecture at the National University of Ireland, to draft working drawings for the restoration of the tower, and these were followed by the local builder, Thomas Rafferty (to whom Yeats, no doubt conflating him with the local poet, referred as "Raftery"). Scott also designed the furniture, which was made by a carpenter in Gort but assembled on the spot because the stairways were too narrow to accommodate large pieces. The work proceeded steadily but slowly. During the summer of 1918 Yeats and his new wife stayed at Ballinamantane House in nearby Gort while construction continued with materials acquired from an old mill—beams and thick planks and paving stones. The tower was covered by a flat concrete roof because the builders feared that the gales from the Atlantic would tear off the more elaborate slate roof that had been designed. In July Yeats wrote a poem describing the project and laying a curse on his heirs should they alter, for trivial reasons, "What Raftery built and Scott designed."[11] When the poem was later published (in *Michael Robartes and the Dancer*, 1921), he deleted the specific allusions to the builder and architect and softened the ominous ending from a curse to a wish:

> I, the poet William Yeats,
> With old mill boards and sea-green slates,
> And smithy work from the Gort forge,
> Restored this tower for my wife George;
> And may these characters remain
> When all is ruin once again.

In point of fact, it was another year before Yeats was able to move his family into the tower, and the work of restoration continued floor by floor for several more years, as a first-floor living room was added to the ground-floor dining room and, by 1922, a bedroom on the second floor. The guest room or "Strangers' Room" on the third floor, which Yeats had initially planned as a room for study and meditation, remained unfinished.

When we consider the difficulties associated with the move into Thoor Ballylee—the expensive roof repairs, the need to have much of the furniture carpentered in situ because of the narrow stairway, the primitive sanitation, the constant flooding and dampness that finally drove the family out again—we are justified in assuming that it must have been a powerful compulsion that prompted Yeats to acquire the property. Indeed, the purchase was regarded as such a folly by his friends that Ezra Pound wickedly remarked that Yeats had undertaken his lecture tour to America in 1920 "to make enough to buy a few shingles for his phallic symbol on the Bogs. Ballyphallus or whatever he calls it with the river on the first floor."[12]

◨ 3 ◨

Pound was not entirely off the mark. Yeats was obsessed with towers even before he laid eyes on Thoor Ballylee. In his essay "The Philosophy of Shelley's Poetry" (1900) he stressed the importance of towers in that romantic oeuvre:

The tower, important in Maeterlinck, as in Shelley, is, like the sea, and rivers, and caves with fountains, a very ancient symbol, and would perhaps, as years went by, have grown more important in his poetry. The contrast between it and the cave in *Laon and Cyntha* suggests a contrast between the mind looking outward upon men and things and the mind looking inward upon itself, which may or may not have been in Shelley's mind, but certainly helps, with one knows not how many other dim meanings, to give the poem mystery and shadow. It is only by ancient symbols, by symbols that have numberless meanings besides the one or two the writer lays an emphasis upon, or the half-score he knows of, that any highly subjective art can escape from the barrenness and shallowness of a too conscious arrangement, into the abundance and depth of Nature.[13]

Yeats returned again and again to the image of Shelley's Prince Athanase, who "follow[s] his mysterious studies in a lighted tower above the sea,"[14] recalling in 1906 the "solitary light burning in the tower of Prince Athanase."[15] Writing many years later from his own tower, Yeats suggested that "Shelley's dream of a young man, his hair blanched with sorrow, studying philosophy in some lonely tower"[16] appealed to him so powerfully because, in accordance with his theory of masks, it contrasted so drastically with his own "gregarious" nature. In addition to Prince Athanase and Maeterlinck's *Princesse Maleine*, Yeats had also been impressed by the tower scene in Villiers de l'Isle-Adam's *Axël*, which he had read ("slowly and laboriously as one reads a sacred book—my French was very bad")[17] before he went to Paris in 1894 and attended a performance of the symbolist classic. In the introduction to the Jarrold translation of 1925 Yeats mused: "Is it only because I opened the book for the first time when I had vivid senses of youth that I must see that tower room always and hear always that thunder?"[18] From the start, then, Yeats regarded towers as an easily recognizable literary image for the retreat of poets and thinkers. Reporting on his walking tour of Italy in 1907, Yeats described a vision he experienced on the road to Urbino, triggered by his view of a distant tower: "I saw suddenly in the mind's eye an old man, erect and a little gaunt, standing in the door of the tower, while about him broke a windy light.

He was the poet who had at last, because he had done so much for the word's sake, come to share in the dignity of the saint."[19]

Even before he moved into his tower, then, Yeats was haunted by the associations of spirituality and introspection that had been linked with towers from Milton and Shelley down to the French symbolists. He was of course familiar with other traditional associations of towers and mountains. In his early poetry, as in *The Wanderings of Oisin* (1889), "dark towers" (363, 369) represent nothing more than a conventional romantic locale. He later alludes several times (109, 328) to the "topless towers" of Troy associated leitmotivically with Helen. He is acquainted with the astronomical function of the "starry towers of Babylon" (216). Yeats's most profoundly pessimistic insights into the transitoriness of civilization are attributed to hermits on the sacred mountain in "Meru" (1934). The late poem "Lapis Lazuli" (1936) features Chinese sages who ascend a mountain to contemplate "all the tragic scene" of life and to hearken to "mournful melodies" (293). And the verse drama *The Herne's Egg* (1938) exploits the ancient association of mountaintops with the sacred priestess when Attracta ascends the mountain to couple with the Great Herne. Several of these associations are linked in "Blood and the Moon," where Yeats writes:

> Alexandria's was a beacon tower, and Babylon's
> An image of the moving heavens, a log-book of the
>   sun's journey and the moon's;
> And Shelley had his towers, thought's crowned
>   powers he called them once.   (233)

But for Yeats, at least initially, Thoor Ballylee was almost exclusively the solitary poet's tower of English literary tradition. The first poem that specifically mentions Thoor Ballylee, written even before Yeats had acquired the property, features the configuration of tower, lamp, and book familiar from Milton and Shelley: in "Ego Dominus Tuus" (1915) *Hic* describes "the grey sand beside the shallow stream / Under your old wind-beaten tower, where still / A lamp burns on beside the open book / That Michael Robartes left . . ." (157). At this point Yeats is not yet ready to assume the mask of the mysterious student of the occult, Robartes, whom he had depicted in *Rosa Alchemica* (1897). When *Hic* asks why *Ille* has left the lamp "burning alone beside an open book" to come outside and trace characters upon the sands, *Ille* replies in words that anticipate Yeats's own self-analysis in "The Trembling of the Veil" (1922):[20]

> Because I seek an image, not a book,
> Those men that in their writings are most wise
> Own nothing but their blind, stupefied hearts.
>
> (159)

In other words, Yeats is not yet ready to enter the tower of introspection.

Precisely the same cluster of images, with the sources now specified, occurs in "The Phases of the Moon," written three years later (1918) when Yeats already owned Thoor Ballylee but had not yet actually moved in. However, he projects his poetic self into the tower, where he occupies himself with the images rejected earlier by *Ille*. As Aherne and Robartes, the two masks into which Yeats divided his character, stand on the bridge looking up at the tower, Robartes observes:

We are on the bridge; that shadow is the tower,
And the light proves that he is reading still.
He has found, after the manner of his kind,
Mere images; chosen this place to live in
Because, it may be, of the candle-light
From the far tower where Milton's Platonist
Sat late, or Shelley's visionary prince:
The lonely light that Samuel Palmer engraved,
An image of mysterious wisdom won by toil. . . .

(161)

At the end of the poem, the two personae are still standing outside; but, as a bat wheels around them with its
squeaky cry, "The light in the tower window was put out"
(164)—a sign that the poet has concluded his poem, a
totality embracing not only the two figures on the bridge
below but also the poet in his tower.[21]

It is characteristic of the other four poems written before the move into the tower in the summer of 1919 that
they all, like the two just cited, are written from a stand-
point outside the tower, and that they restrict themselves
to conventional literary associations. The elegy "In Memory of Major Robert Gregory" (1918) recalls that Gregory,
who had encouraged Yeats to acquire "The tower set on
the stream's edge" (131), is among the friends who will be
prevented by death from joining him there "Beside a fire
of turf in th'ancient tower" and talking until late hours
before climbing up "the narrow winding stairs to bed"
(130). Similarly, "A Prayer on Going into My House"
(1918) refers to the tower that is about to be, but is not
yet, occupied. The poet invokes God's blessing on his
tower and on his heirs, provided they remain unspoiled,
and suggests that he himself, during the summer months

that he will spend there, will be in touch with traditional values—both objects and, implicitly, ideas—that he has taken as his new standard or "norm" (168). As he wrote in the summer of 1918, "I am making a setting for my old age, a place to influence lawless youth, with its severity and antiquity."[22] Even at this point Yeats recognized the impermanence of mere physical reality in comparison with the endurance of the poetic word, as he implied in his inscription for the tower: "And may these characters remain / When all is ruin once again" (188). But in the mood of departure and change with which he moved into his tower, he dared to hope that his tower would come to represent the beauty, innocence, and tradition that he was invoking in his writings of those years.

Finally, in "A Prayer for My Daughter" (June 1919), as "the sea-wind scream[s] upon the tower" (185), the poet thinks of his child sleeping in her cradle and prays for the gifts he wishes for her: beauty, but not the destructive beauty of Helen of Troy; intelligence without the "intellectual hatred" of Maud Gonne; charm and constancy; and "radical innocence." In conclusion, he hopes that she will marry into a house not unlike the one that he anticipates establishing at Thoor Ballylee, "Where all's accustomed, ceremonious" (187).

Very early, then, Yeats regarded his tower as more than a habitation: it was being transformed into a symbol. Writing in 1919, he noted that the tower needed "another year's work under our own eyes before it is a fitting monument and symbol."[23] At first, as viewed from without, it represented essentially a poetic and philosophical retreat after the fashion of Milton, Shelley, and the French symbolists. Having once occupied the premises, however, he recognized its potential also as a haven of the traditional Anglo-Irish values of ceremony and innocence, the "embattled values"[24] being destroyed by the political forces that had come to power during the Troubles following the Easter Rising. In sum, Thoor Ballylee exemplifies essentially the Proud Tower of the pre-1914 world, especially as it occurred in Anglo-Ireland. As he wrote to John Quinn shortly after moving in: "Ballylee is a good house for a child to grow up in—a place full of history and romance, with plenty to do every day."[25]

▣ 4 ▣

Once installed in the tower, however, which he and his family occupied intermittently for several summers from 1919 to 1929, Yeats began to see further symbolic dimensions in his new habitation. To be sure, Yeats had a large supply of symbols in his poetic arsenal. In 1921 he summarized, "My main symbols are Sun and Moon (in all phases), Tower, Mask, Tree (Tree with Mask hanging on the trunk), Well."[26] Sometimes the tower occurs in close conjunction with other images: notably the bridge and the river.[27] Yet almost no other symbol lets us trace so clearly as the tower the emergence in the poet's mind of a private image from a traditional one.[28] This process is evident especially in the parallel volumes *The Tower* (1928) and *The Winding Stair* (1933), both of which thematize the tower and use its image for their frontispieces.[29]

We first note the change in the seven-poem cycle of "Meditations in Time of Civil War" (1922), the first poem written explicitly "about Ballylee"[30] after the earlier group of six tower poems. In April 1922, following a two-and-a-half-year absence, Yeats returned to Thoor Ballylee, wondering whether literature would be much changed by "that most momentous of events, the return of evil"[31]—an insight reflected by the "bitterness" of the poems written at that time, which astonished him when he reread *The Tower* shortly after its publication.[32] Following a general meditation on "Ancestral Houses," which introduces the theme of tradition, the second poem, "My House," describes in detail the setting of Yeats's new dwelling:

> An ancient bridge, and a more ancient tower,
> A farmhouse that is sheltered by its wall,
> An acre of stony ground,
> Where the symbolic rose can break in flower,
> Old ragged elms, old thorns innumerable. . . .
>
> (199)

Beginning, like all the earlier tower poems, on the outside, the cycle as a whole goes on to provide what amounts to a guided tour of the tower, leading us gradually up the winding stair to the battlements atop the building. The second strophe takes us inside the tower but depicts the interior in terms that do not yet go beyond the familiar Miltonic tradition within which he was locating himself—tower, lamp, and book:

> A winding stair, a chamber arched with stone,
> A grey stone fireplace with an open hearth,
> A candle and written page.
> *Il Penseroso's* Platonist toiled on
> In some like chamber. . . .
>
> (199)

But the next strophe adds for the first time a new element: the historical reference to the "man-at-arms" who "spent his days / In this tumultuous spot" introduces an analogy between past and present in which Yeats himself represents the modern pole. The third section describes "My Table," upon which lie the poet's tools, his pen and paper, as well as "Sato's gift," the sword presented to him by Junzo Sato two years earlier during his American tour. "My Descendants" picks up the theme of heritage introduced in "A Prayer for My Daughter," but this time in a minor key. Yeats realizes that the vigor of the family may play itself out in his daughter and son. In that case, the tower through its decay may become an appropriate symbol for the decline of the family, should his descendants lose their vigor "Through natural declension of the soul," obsession with the trivialities of the present, or bad marriages.

> May this laborious stair and this stark tower
> Become a roofless ruin that the owl
> May build in the cracked masonry and cry
> Her desolation to the desolate sky. (201)

Yet whether they flourish or decline, "These stones remain their monument and mine." The tower, no longer simply the traditional symbol, has suddenly become an intimately personal image for the poet and his family. As such it offers a place of refuge from the civil war raging outside.

At the time he was composing his "Meditations" Yeats wrote to Olivia Shakespear: "As I have not seen a paper for days I do not know how far we have plunged into civil war but it will hardly disturb us here."[33] Yeats informs us in his notes to the poem (455) that on one night during

57

this period the IRA blew up the "ancient bridge" and forbade the family to leave the house, "but were otherwise polite." This incident underlies the section "The Road at My Door," in which "An affable Irregular" appears at the door and discusses the weather with the poet, who afterwards "turn[s] toward my chamber, caught / In the cold snows of a dream" (202). The isolation of the tower, as well as the political ambivalence of its Anglo-Irish inhabitants, is made even plainer in the next section, "The Stare's Nest by My Window." As the poet (for the first time in his tower poems) ascends the winding stair, he notes the "crevices / Of loosening masonry," where the stares (starlings) have built their nests. Now that the birds have fled, like the "Wild Geese" mentioned three years earlier, leaving the nest (Ireland) empty, the poet invites the honeybees, those traditional symbols of soul, to come and build their hive "in the empty house of the stare" (202).[34]

The high balustrade is (again for the first time) the setting of the final poem, where the poet "climb[s] to the tower-top and lean[s] upon broken stone" (203) to meditate upon the hatred stirred up by the civil war. As he gazes across the misty valley, "Monstrous familiar images swim to the mind's eye": cries of vengeance as a "fit symbol for those who labour from hatred, and so for sterility in various kinds" (455); delightful visions of ladies borne by cloud-pale unicorns (that is, the cultivated past), who must "give place to an indifferent multitude, give place /To brazen hawks" (Yeats's image for the gloomy bird of prey that follows the straight road of logic [455]). Yet although the poet has now moved into the tower and climbed to the top, he is not yet capable of making the leap from the balustrades into the visionary cosmos.

Turning away from his mixed visions, he shuts the door to the tower and goes back down the winding stair, asking himself whether a more active career with accomplishments more readily understood by the multitude would have better satisfied his ambitious heart. But he concludes that the secluded satisfactions of poetry and thought, for which his tower is the appropriate site, are his destined lot—a poetry and thought now informed, however, not simply by Plato's pages but also by images from his own life and Irish history. (It is worth noting the irony that, later that same year, Yeats accepted the invitation to become a senator in the new Irish Republic and, only a year later, received the Nobel Prize. "Something that all others understand" with a vengeance!)

This insight, coupled with the increasingly obtrusive problem of age, is further developed three years later in the title-poem of the volume, "The Tower" (written in October 1925). *The Tower* is above all a book recording the transition from maturity to what Yeats, in his sixtieth year, regarded as senility. The great poem that opens the volume, "Sailing to Byzantium" (1927), chronicles this shift. The poet recognizes that the modern world "is no country for old men." And so he makes his way to Byzantium where, "studying / Monuments of its own magnificence," his soul can rid itself of its earthbound heart and be gathered "into the artifice of eternity."

The tower at Ballylee now becomes Yeats's personal Byzantium, his retreat "out of nature" and away from his new responsibilities as the "smiling public man" (213) depicted in "Among School Children" to a place where he can "sing . . . Of what is past, or passing, or to come" (192)—that is, of the Irish past, his own present, and the future of his heirs. The title-poem, which follows directly upon "Sailing to Byzantium," takes up the theme of "this absurdity," the decrepit old age that has been tied to him as, in the concluding image, a kettle to a dog's tail. Never, not even in boyhood, has his imagination been more active. But the public expects the aging writer to forsake poetry and youthful passion in favor of philosophical speculation, the traditional pursuits of the Miltonic and Shelleyan tower:

> It seems that I must bid the Muse go pack,
> Choose Plato and Plotinus for a friend
> Until imagination, ear and eye,
> Can be content with argument and deal
> In abstract things; or be derided by
> A sort of battered kettle at the heel.   (192)

In his frustration the poet ascends directly (without the extensive tour of "Meditations") to the top of his tower, where he paces upon the battlements "And send[s] imagination forth" to summon up images and memories from the surrounding countryside. The landscape responds, flooding his imagination with scenes from the history of Ballylee:[35] of Mrs. French, who lived near Ballylee in the eighteenth century and whose servant once clipped off the ears of a farmer who had been insolent to her; of the peasant beauty Mary Hynes, for love of whom one man was drowned in the great bog of Cloone; of the bard Raftery, blind like Homer himself, whose songs about Mary Hynes "had driven their wits astray"; and of the hero of Yeats's own *Stories of Red Hanrahan* (1897). These semimythic memories gradually give way to more specific historical figures, "in the Great Memory stored" (194), that intrude into the poet's consciousness like archetypes from the collective memory of the tower. Wondering if all those ancient figures raged "As I do now against old age," Yeats dismisses them, keeping behind only Hanrahan, "For I need all his mighty memories" (195). The thought of that "old lecher" brings the poet back to the present and to his own reflections upon a woman won and lost.

The first part of "The Tower" concerns the poet's present and his worries about age and loss of imagination, while the second part summons forth the past out of imagination. The third part now turns to the future: "It is time that I wrote my will." To posterity Yeats bequeaths his pride, inherited from the people of Burke and Grattan, "Bound neither to Cause nor to State" (196). With that resolution Yeats also resolves the dilemma of the first section: he refuses to be bound, even in age, by the simple polarities of poetry or philosophy, life or abstraction. Now that his vision has enabled him to attain a psychic state where all oppositions are nullified, where life and death have not yet been polarized, "I mock Plotinus' thought / And cry in Plato's teeth" (196).

That humankind through its collective dreams creates a "Translunar Paradise" is the poet's final insight from the battlements of his tower and his bequest of faith and pride. Returning to the imagery of "Sailing to Byzantium," the poet resolves to commit himself to poetry, the means through which by an almost alchemical transmutation the fleeting experiences of transitory life can be rendered into the permanence of art.

The tower, in sum, is no longer simply the Miltonian place of Platonic meditation or the emblem of his own family and Ireland: it has become the privileged locus where Yeats attains a loftier state of awareness in which he is for the first time capable of reconciling at least tentatively the antinomies that have hitherto vexed him: *vita activa* and *vita contemplativa*, action and dream, present and past, power and knowledge, Aherne and Robartes, *Hic* and *Ille*, Soul and Self, and all the other seemingly irreconcilable masks of his earlier poetry. As he wrote to Sturge Moore, who had just designed the frontispiece for *The Tower*, which at Yeats's request was to "suggest the real object": "I like to think of that building as a permanent symbol of my work plainly visible to the passer-by. As you know, all my art theories depend upon just this— rooting of mythology in the earth."[36]

◨ 5 ◨

If it was the culminating insight of "The Tower" (and *The Tower*) that antinomies can be reconciled, then it was the challenge of the next volume, *The Winding Stair* (1933), not only to give shape to that insight but also to add another dimension to his image.[37] The prevailing image in *The Tower* was the tower itself, from whose battlements the poet could look out and survey not only space but also time. In *The Winding Stair* that image is internalized. The narrow stairway that winds, as in Renaissance depictions of the Tower of Babel, around the inside of the tower, becomes an image of the poet himself as he makes his way, in ever widening gyres, up the stairs of consciousness. (The winding stair had been mentioned in several earlier poems—e.g., "In Memory of Major Robert Gregory" and "My House"—but with no symbolic significance.) As Yeats stated in his notes to the volume, "In this book and elsewhere, I have used towers, and one tower in particular, as symbols and have compared their winding stairs to the philosophical gyres" (456). Yeats goes on, misleadingly, to suggest that this new dimension is implicit in the traditional romantic image: "it is hardly necessary to interpret what comes from the main track of thought and expression. Shelley uses towers constantly as symbols, and there are gyres in Swedenborg, and in Thomas Aquinas and certain classical authors." Perhaps so. But the combination of towers with the theory of gyres, which Yeats had developed in *The Vision* (1925), is unique to Yeats. Indeed, the interpenetrating cones, which he used to illustrate his theory, suggest in their very appearance a tower. There was nothing in Milton, Shelley, or the French symbolists to evoke this association.

As in the preceding volume, the tower is the dominant image in three major poems of *The Winding Stair*, all written from Thoor Ballylee in 1927—"a new Tower series" to which Yeats remarks that he was "partly driven" by the murder on 10 July of Kevin O'Higgins, vice president and minister for justice.[38] In "Blood and the Moon" written that summer, the tower itself becomes a symbol for the reconciliation of power and knowledge—so powerfully, indeed, that Yeats was accused of fascist leanings. Certainly, here, his antidemocratic tendencies, which had been growing stronger in the course of some twenty years, reach a first high point, to be followed by the distinct fascist sympathies of the 1930s.[39] Yeats points out that the walls of his tower, for which he invokes a blessing, rose "from these / Storm-beaten cottages" (232) in an age when the Norman invaders conquered the Gaelic inhabitants of Ireland. He states that he has chosen the "powerful emblem" of the tower specifically as an ironic reminder, in a debilitated age, of stronger, more vigorous ages and "In mockery of a time / Half dead at the top"

(233). Again the climb up the winding stairway leads the poet along a Babylonian spiritual ascent of consciousness that removes him from the commonplace and, in the second part, puts him in touch with an older, more authentic tradition. Having recalled the towers of Alexandria and Babylon as well as Shelley's "crowned powers," he continues:

> I declare this tower is my symbol; I declare
> This winding, gyring, spiring treadmill of a stair is
>   my ancestral stair;
> That Goldsmith and the Dean, Berkeley and Burke
>   have travelled there.   (233)

Those four incantational names evoke for Yeats (as in "The Seven Sages" and elsewhere) precisely the great Protestant Anglo-Irish tradition of intellect and spirituality[40] that, tormented by its own ambivalence between violence and vision, between "blood" and "moon," has been lost in the political confusions of the present. Swift is torn between the two poles of his being because "the heart in his blood-sodden breast had dragged him down into mankind"; Goldsmith sips at "the honey-pot of his mind"; Burke is "haughtier-headed"; and "God-appointed Berkeley" sought to overcome the dilemma by proclaiming that "this pragmatical, preposterous pig of a world" is nothing but a transitory dream.

In Yeats's tower, past and future, action and thought, blood and moon come together at least for a moment and in a vision. Following this brief epiphany, however, section 3 returns the poet harshly to the present. Soldier, assassin, and executioner have stood on the blood-saturated ground of the tower; but it has been washed clean in the course of seven centuries, and now "the purity of the unclouded moon" illuminates it. But the compromise cannot last; the tower decays, like the individual too weak to hold the antinomies together. Wisdom (the achievement of the dead) and power (the property of the living) are destined to remain incompatible, as the fourth section concludes gloomily. "Is every modern nation like the tower, / Half dead at the top?" (234). Yet the ideal itself remains unstained by mere reality.

The tower figures importantly in another poem written that year, "Symbols," in whose three haiku-like strophes Yeats simply lists his central images: Sato's sword, its sheath of embroidered silk, and "A storm-beaten old watch-tower" (235). The brief poem amounts virtually to a précis of the longer "Dialogue of Self and Soul" (1927), which was originally called simply "Sword and Tower" and in which the tower is vividly identified with the poet's own soul. Here Soul summons the Self "to the winding ancient stair" that curls around the tower like the ascent of Bruegel's Tower of Babel:

> Set all your mind upon the steep ascent,
> Upon the broken, crumbling battlement. . . .
>
> (230)

The role of the tower as the symbolic link between man and eternity is made quite clear, the springboard from which the imagination can vault into the heavens. But this time, in Yeats's poetic dialectics, Self has the final word.[41] As they ascend, they fix their eyes, far beyond the tower's broken top, "Upon the star that marks the hidden pole" where all thought is done and one can no longer distinguish darkness from the soul. Like the Babylonian astronomers, the watcher on the tower has the privilege of gazing into eternity. But Self, like the hero of a symbolist drama, rejects the lure of spirituality and introspection, clinging to his sword in its embroidered case. Soul asks why the imagination of a man long past his prime should remember things that are "emblematical of love and war." But Self sets its "emblems of the day against the tower / Emblematical of the night" (231). Again the Soul proposes the tower as the ascent to Heaven, to the realm of the Platonic ideas where Being can be distinguished from Reality, "*Is* from the *Ought,* or *Knower* from the *Known*" (231). At this point, however, Self wins the debate: the second part is no longer a dialogue, but a monologue in which Self praises life in all its inadequacy, where blind men stumble into impure ditches: "Everything we look upon is blest" (232). With this poem, then, the image of the tower moves yet another spiral up the gyre: from traditional image of the poetic self by way of emblem of family and nation to a cosmic reminder of eternity. With the tower, perhaps more than with any other of his principal images, Yeats succeeded in locating himself in a tradition that was not just literary but also mythic, with associations extending back to ancient Babylonia.

◙ 6 ◙

Despite Yeats's recognition in 1922 ("Meditations in Time of Civil War") that his descendants might not maintain their vigor, and that the tower and its winding stair might become a ruin symbolic of the family's deterioration, he still insisted that "These stones remain their monument and mine" (201). While the tower no longer commanded such an obsessively central position after the last summer that Yeats spent at Thoor Ballylee in 1929, it remained a presence in his poetry. The allusions can be quite tenuous, as in the late poem "The Statues" (1938), which in accordance with the theory of art developed in *A Vision* sets the ordered beauty of Phidias's sculpture against the chaos of the Asiatic world and establishes an implicit parallel between the Greek defeat of the Persians at Salamis and the political situation in contemporary Europe.[42] In the last strophe, after Yeats has made his way from Greek antiquity by way of the Middle Ages down to the present, he arrives at the Easter Rising of 1916 and speaks of the Irish, who have a claim to a glorious past but have degenerated into "formless spawning fury," the rapidly reproducing mobs of modern democracy. In the last two verses, using an image that recalls the first strophe of "A Dialogue of Self and Soul," Yeats expresses his hope that his people may once again "Climb to our proper dark" (323)—an image of ascension resonant of his tower poems—to a point at which they will be able to reanimate a lifeless past rigidified into mere monuments.

It is fitting that Yeats's last poem, written on 21 January 1939, only a week before his death, should return one final time to that dominant image. "The Black Tower" is no longer simply a private icon but a general symbol for the incorruptible guardians of the Proud Tower.[43] Poor, subsisting on modest food and sour wine, they remain "oath-bound"—that is, loyal to the aristocratic past represented by the tower whose ancient rulers stand upright in their tombs. True to those values, they resist "Those banners come to bribe or threaten"—that is, the political forces that threaten the individual, Ireland, or Europe itself at the end of the 1930s. Alone among them, the old cook (the poet himself), though called a fool by the others, "swears that he hears the king's great horn"—the values of the the Irish past, both Celtic and Anglo-Irish. As he put it in a passage of "Pages from a Diary in 1930" that amounts to a commentary on the poem:

> Preserve that which is living and help the two Irelands, Gaelic Ireland and Anglo-Ireland, so to unite that neither shall shed its pride. Study the great problems of the world, as they have been lived in our scenery, the re-birth of European spirituality in the mind of Berkeley, the restoration of European order in the mind of Burke. Every nation is the whole world in a mirror and our mirror has twice been very bright and clear.[44]

In the course of some forty years, then, Yeats's image of the tower developed from a conventional romantic topos (tower, lamp, book) first to an icon for the retreat of the poet and his immediate family, then to an emblem for Ireland, next to a symbol of human consciousness, maturing in the winding gyres of its stairway, and finally, on its ramparts, to a springboard into the cosmos. The turning point from conventional topos to a larger image came almost precisely at the moment when Yeats purchased and moved into Thoor Ballylee: the stages of its development correspond with great precision to the periods of extended stay at Ballylee (1919, 1922, 1926, and 1927). As long as he stood outside, the tower remained the lonely tower of the romantic poet stooped over his Plato. Once he entered its premises, the spiraling ascent to the top and the view from the battlements over time and space afforded the perspectives from which the tower could become its own "monument of unageing intellect."

CHAPTER THREE

Robinson Jeffers:
The Tower beyond Time

Fig. 13. Hawk Tower. Photographer, John H. Gamble.
Permission of Robinson Jeffers Tor House Foundation.

▣ 1 ▣

On his first trip to Ireland in 1929, Robinson Jeffers (1887–1962) twice visited the tower at Ballylee, which Yeats had only recently vacated. "The place was as beautiful and lonely as it ought to be. Yeats wasn't there; nobody was, all the shutters up, so we could wander around freely. I'd like to go back there sometime, it was very lovely."[1] During the six months that Jeffers with his wife and two sons spent in Ireland and England on that occasion, as he wrote to his patron Albert Bender, the family visited some twenty round towers all over Ireland.[2] The poems that he composed during that trip and collected under the title *Descent to the Dead* (1929) amount to a veritable paean to the stone structures of the British Isles, from the primitive dolmens and megalithic burial mounds and prehistoric stone circles down to the round towers associated with the early Christian churches. So captivated was Jeffers by the Irish edifices that he indicated, only half in jest, his intention to "begin building a round tower or something" as soon as he got back home to California.[3] A round stone tower would have been perfectly consistent with Jeffers's project on a promontory just south of Carmel, where since 1919 he had been engaged in building a stone habitation whose elaboration would occupy most of his afternoons for the next thirty years. But it would also have been de trop since the complex already included one tower—Hawk Tower, a forty-foot four-story square edifice overlooking the Pacific.

Unlike Yeats and (as we shall see) Rilke, Jeffers was not drawn to towers as the actualization of an image that had long been present in his thought and work. Towers play no role whatsoever in the first two rather pedestrian volumes of conventional verse that he published: *Flagons and Apples* (1912) and *Californians* (1916). His poetic breakthrough, along with the emergence of the tower as a governing image, in *Tamar* (1924) and in his arguably finest and certainly most popular work, *Roan Stallion, Tamar and Other Poems* (1925),[4] resulted directly from experiences connected with the building of his own tower at Carmel.

In the foreword to his *Selected Poetry* Jeffers observed that two accidents changed and directed his life: his marriage and his move to the Monterey coast mountains. It was 1906 when Jeffers met his future wife, whom he later characterized as "more like a woman in a Scotch ballad, passionate, untamed and rather heroic—or like a falcon—than like any ordinary person."[5] The product of a highly eccentric education—his father, a professor of biblical languages and ecclesiastical history, taught him Latin and Greek at an early age, and for several years he moved from school to school in Switzerland and Germany, mastering French and German—Jeffers had recently graduated from Occidental College in Los Angeles at age eighteen and was taking graduate courses in literature at the University of Southern California.[6] Una Call Kuster, two years his elder, had interrupted her college years at Berkeley to marry a successful attorney and was now continuing her education at USC. The aspiring young poet and the spirited young matron, whose intellectual ambitions were not satisfied by the country-club life of southern California, met in a German course, where they read Goethe's *Faust.* The friendship, purely intellectual at first, was maintained by correspondence in 1906 when Jeffers returned to Europe and the University of Zurich to continue his studies. Not content to pursue a degree in the humanities, the restless Jeffers broke off his studies after a semester and returned to Los Angeles, where he spent a year translating German medical papers and then, in 1907, enrolled in the medical school at USC, where the relationship with Una was more intensively resumed. Despite academic success and recognition by his professors, Jeffers left medical school in 1910 without a degree and moved to Seattle to enter the School of Forestry at the University of Washington—and also hoping that separation might resolve an affair that had grown increasingly problematic. Rapidly dismayed by the mercantile aspects of forestry, Jeffers again broke off his studies and returned the following summer to southern California, where he almost immediately encountered Una again and resumed their relationship. This time the affair became so obvious that rumors reached her husband, who asked her to go to Europe for a year in order to sort things out. However, the trip afforded nothing more than a delay of the inevitable. Shortly after Una's return in November 1912, the Kusters went through divorce proceedings that were widely commented upon in the society section of the Los Angeles newspapers. In August 1913, Jeffers and Una were married.

The new couple planned initially to move to Europe— partly, no doubt, to escape the scandal and gossip at home. But when Una became pregnant, they decided to await the birth of the child. When their daughter died the following May only a day after birth, the plans for a European exile were again thwarted—this time by the war. In

September 1914, therefore, seeking a quiet retreat for their lives and work, they followed a friend's advice and took a stagecoach north to Carmel.

Carmel, the site of one of Father Junípero Serra's missions, had attracted writers ever since Robert Louis Stevenson took its beaches as the setting for *Treasure Island* (1883). For the decade preceding World War I, it had provided the center for a large colony of California writers as well as such visitors as Upton Sinclair and Sinclair Lewis.[7] By the time the Jefferses arrived, the heyday of Carmel's *vie de bohème* was past. But that had little meaning for Jeffers with his love of solitude. What attracted him to the Monterey coast was something entirely different from any modern sophistication.

> For the first time in my life I could see people living— amid magnificent unspoiled scenery—essentially as they did in the Idyls or the Sagas, or in Homer's Ithaca. Here was life purged of its ephemeral accretions. Men were riding after cattle, or plowing the headland, hovered by white sea-gulls, as they have done for thousands of years, and will for thousands of years to come. Here was contemporary life that was also permanent life; and not shut from the modern world but conscious of it and related to it; capable of expressing its spirit, but unencumbered by the mass of poetically irrelevant details and complexities that make a civilization.[8]

At first the couple rented a small cabin in the village and then, early in 1917 after the birth of their twin boys, a larger cottage in a pine forest nearby. But convinced that they wanted to spend their lives in Carmel, they thought about more permanent solutions. At one point they contemplated building a house from the "chalky" stone used at Father Serra's mission and even planned to call the place their Tour d'Ivoire.[9] Certainly, a fin de siècle ivory tower would have been consistent with the conventional poetry that Jeffers had written up to that time. Then in 1919 they bought a plot of land at Mission Point, a barren hill overlooking the ocean two miles south of the village, which had long been one of their favorite picnic spots, and which reminded them, as Una wrote, of the rocky promontories, known as "tors," that she had seen in England.[10] This became the location for Tor House, which was modeled after an old Tudor barn that Una had seen in Surrey during her trip to Europe in 1912.

▣ 2 ▣

Deciding to use granite rather than the softer chalkstone found in Father Serra's mission, they hired a contractor and a stonemason from Monterey and hauled the heavy boulders up a chute from the beach fifty yards below. Working with the stonecutters and masons—he was entrusted only with such simple chores as mixing mortar and carrying the hod—Jeffers not only learned the craft of stonemasonry; he also came to love stone itself and to appreciate the artisanship of those who work with it. As he wrote at the time in the poem "To the Stone-Cutters" (from *Tamar*, 1924), stonecutters, "fighting time with marble," are not unlike the poet, who also "Builds his monument mockingly." For humankind will die out along with the "blithe earth" of flora and fauna. "Yet stones have stood for a thousand years, and pained thoughts found / The honey of peace in old poems"

Fig. 14. Hawk Tower and Tor House. Photographer, Jessica B. Malikowski. Permission of Robinson Jeffers Tor House Foundation.

(1:5).[11] Already here—with its Horatian conclusion comparing the lasting quality of poetry to that of nature[12]—the hallmarks of Jeffers's mature poetry are evident: the distinctive unrhymed long line; the strong narrative impulse; the attempt to present aspects of everyday life and to express philosophical ideas in verse—in short, the ambition to "reclaim some of the power and reality that [modernist poetry] was so hastily surrendering to prose."[13] Above all, we find here Jeffers's pervasive, even obsessive, theme: the perdurance of nature, and especially stone, as opposed to a very transitory human civilization. As Una explained fifteen years later, Jeffers underwent in 1919 a mystical awakening of the sort that religious converts are said to experience.[14] Various factors were involved: the death in 1914 of his father, to whom he had been bound in a tense love-hate relationship; his frustrations resulting from his hitherto unsuccessful poetic career; and conflicts with Una caused by his wish to enlist during the war. "Another factor was the building of Tor House. As he helped the masons shift and place the wind and wave-worn granite I think he realized some kinship with it and became aware of strengths in himself unknown before."

This obsession with stone, which often amounts to a mystical identification, pervaded his poetry for the next forty years. In the volume *Tamar* (1924) he wrote an apostrophe "To the Rock That Will Be a Cornerstone of the House":

> Lend me the stone strength of the past and I will
>   lend you
> The wings of the future, for I have them.
> How dear you will be to me when I too grow old,
>   old comrade.   (1:11)

In "On Building with Stone" (in *Cawdor*, 1928) Jeffers maintained that stonework is "a far sweeter toil" than writing poetry. "I'd liefer bed one boulder in the house-wall than be the time's / Archilochus" (1:394). In "The Old Stone-Mason" (in *Hungerfield*, 1954) the poet personifies the stones of his house that "rolled in the sea for a thousand years" and then "climbed the cliff and stand stiff-ranked in the house-walls" (3:372). As one who has also escaped a foolish, chattering society and taken a stand on principle, he believes that he has much in common with these old rockheads. In another poem ("Watch the Lights Fade," in *Be Angry at the Sun*, 1941) the poet stands on his seaside cliff "like an old stone" while the war rages in Europe and Asia, pondering the inevitable doom of the world.

How soon? Four years or forty?
Why should an old stone pick at the future?
Stand on your shore, old stone, be still while the
Sea-wind salts your head white.   (3:10)

And in one of his most characteristic poems, "Rock and Hawk" (from *Solstice*, 1935) Jeffers discovers the appropriate emblem for himself in a falcon perched on the peak of a gray rock on the headland: "Fierce consciousness joined with final / Disinterestedness," "the falcon's Realist eyes [. . .] / Married to the massive / Mysticism of stone" (2:416).

Till the end of his life Jeffers continued to work with stone, adding to the walls around his house stones not only collected from the beach below but also sent by friends from exotic places.[15] When he and Una went on expeditions, he wrote to Mark Van Doren, "we always take home a stone."[16] And a year later: "My wife is as mad about rocks as I am, fortunately, or rather I as she."[17] Before the trip to Ireland Jeffers explained his reluctance to leave home, saying "I am as attached to this rock as if I were a feudal serf with an iron collar."[18] And in 1953, after Una's death, he wrote in dust jacket copy for Random House that his favorite recreation, in addition to dog walking and being a grandfather, was stonemasonry.[19]

�« 3 »

Tor House was completed in August 1919, and following their move into the house—which had no telephone or electricity and was heated by fireplaces and a Franklin stove—Jeffers continued to work a few hours each day, now single-handedly, building first a stone garage and later a wall surrounding the complex as he pondered the verses he would write down the next day. Then Una expressed a desire for a medieval tower like the ones she had seen in Ireland. One of her sons later surmised that she had in mind specifically Yeats's tower at Ballylee,[20] and certainly the square (rather than round) shape of the two towers would suggest that model. For the next five years Jeffers worked on the project, hauling great granite boulders up from the beach. "Hawk Tower," Una later wrote for the *London Poetry Review* (May 1934), "rose out of our dreams of old Irish towers but we have seen in the eyes of our friends as we have so often climbed to the turret with them in the last dozen years, that in many hearts is the mirage of some symbolic tower—citadel, belfry or beacon light."[21]

Jeffers always acknowledged that the tower was Una's idea; at the time he had not yet visited Ireland. Herself of Irish descent and with an Irish name, Una was obsessed with Ireland:[22] she liked to read aloud from such works as Synge's *Riders to the Sea*, and Yeats was her favorite poet, whose complete works were contained in the extensive library at Tor House.[23] (Friends suspected that she even designed and sewed her husband's clothes in such a fashion that he would resemble the Irish poet.)[24] She studied and collected Irish music, which she performed on her piano. And she became an expert on Irish round towers. In the poignant poem "For Una" (from the volume *Be Angry at the Sun*, 1941) he wrote:

> I built her a tower when I was young—
> Sometime she will die—

> I built it with my hands, I hung
> Stones in the sky. (3:33)

As he was working on the tower, Jeffers commented on its progress in letters to friends. He had a Latin inscription cut in marble to set in the parapet, *R. J. suis manibus me turrem falconis fecit* (With his own hands R. J. made me, tower of the falcon), along with hawk gargoyles and a keystone with a hawk carved on it.[25] (The tower was called Hawk Tower after a sparrow hawk that perched daily on the scaffolding as Jeffers was working.) Una wrote that "my little oaken room" on the second floor was decorated with hawks and unicorns, and its mantelpiece bore an inscription from Virgil's *Eclogues: ipsi sibi somnia fingunt.*[26] In a conspicuous ecumenicalism (or even multiculturalism *avant la lettre*) an antique wax figurine of a Spanish or Indian woman—known in the family as the Blessed Virgin of the Tower—stood in a niche in the wall, her back resting against a tile from a Babylonian temple inscribed with a prayer to Ishtar, and facing another niche containing the carved stone head of a heavenly courtesan from the temple at Angkor Wat.[27] Into the wall of the tower Jeffers cemented a bit of the Great Wall of China, a chunk of lava from Vesuvius, a piece of stone from a Cornish cross, and marble from Hadrian's villa, along with other bits and pieces brought by friends or picked up on trips.[28] And other walls of the complex held a fragment of a wall painting from the ruins of Pompeii, some tesserae from the Baths of Caracalla in Rome, a marble carving from Delos, shards from pre-Columbian sites in Central America, and stones from Hradcany Castle in Prague, as well as scores of others.[29]

◘ 4 ◘

During the five years while he was constructing the tower, it became an increasingly obsessive image in his poetry. For Jeffers, as we have seen, the tower was not the realization of an image long present in his poetry: just the opposite! The image of the tower as it emerged in his poetry during the twenties marked a radicalization of the romantic image of the lonely tower of introspection. Yeats, initially brought to his attention by Una as "the greatest living poet,"[30] soon became—along with Shakespeare, Milton, Wordsworth, Shelley, and Tennyson— one of his favorite writers.[31] In 1948 Jeffers heralded Yeats in his great attack on literary modernism entitled "Poetry, Gongorism and a Thousand Years."[32]

> Poetry is not a monologue in a vacuum; it is written in solitude, but it needs to have some sort of audience in mind. Well: there has been a great poet in our time— must I say comparatively great?—an Irishman named Yeats, and he met this problem, but his luck solved it for him. The first half of his life belonged mostly to the specialists, the Celtic Twilight people, the Decadents, even the Gongorists; he was the best among them but not a great poet, and he resented it. He had will and ambition, while Dowson and the others dropped by the wayside. . . .
> But Yeats found in another way his immortality. He was not a firstrate playwright but he had an insuperable will; and when his Ireland changed he was ready. Suddenly in that magic time when a country becomes

a nation, it was Ireland's good fortune that there was a great poet in Ireland. Her unique need, and his will, had produced him.

Jeffers recognized in Yeats's turn from fin de siècle decadence to national mythic statement a parallel to his own literary career. Jeffers had received a sound classical education and, like Yeats, turned to Greek tragedy with translations and adaptations. He also shared Yeats's love of Milton and Shelley. And he found his way to a habitation tower. Unlike Yeats, however, Jeffers had no political ambitions, no faith in humanity's ability to better itself. He was, in an analogy he frequently used, a Cassandra skeptical of political leaders, whether Hitler and Stalin or Churchill and Roosevelt. His tower reveals more of the cold detachment of the *templa serena* of Lucretius, whose work he admired and whose influence on his own thinking he acknowledged.[33] In a letter published in 1935 he wrote:

> It seems to me that in a degenerating society the individual has got to isolate himself morally to a certain extent or else degenerate too. He *can* keep his own morals; he cannot save society's not even though he himself should happen to be Caesar, like Marcus Aurelius (who did all his civic duty and more, but remained isolated in his philosophy, apart from decaying Rome.)[34]

Hawk Tower was the perfect place in which Jeffers could isolate himself from the degenerating society that he saw around him.[35] (It is typical of his withdrawal that Jeffers, so widely traveled in his youth, did not even venture so far afield as San Francisco from 1918 until he needed to go there for a passport in 1929.)

5

The work in which the image of stones and tower emerges in full force—its pervasive stone imagery is unexplainable without reference to the poet's daily stonework—is "The Tower beyond Tragedy," which was written while Jeffers was building his tower and first published in *Roan Stallion, Tamar and Other Poems* (1925). This was Jeffers's first attempt to deal with a classical subject in the form of the long poem—the synthesis of narrative, dramatic, and philosophical modes that has come to be regarded as representative of his oeuvre and his major contribution to twentieth-century American poetry. Hailed upon publication by Mark Van Doren as "undoubtedly one of the great American poems,"[36] it was performed to mixed reviews on Broadway in 1950 by Judith Anderson and enjoyed a notable success in Germany in the 1950s as a radio play in the translation ("Die Quelle") by Eva Hesse.[37] (The ambivalent reception of his works on the stage—"The Tower beyond Tragedy" as well as his adaptations of Euripides' *Medea* and *Hippolytus* [*The Cretan Woman*]—is hardly surprising given the fact that Jeffers claimed in 1958 to have seen no more than six or seven plays in his lifetime.)[38]

Jeffers reported that the play was suggested to him by the "imposing personality" of the Jewish actress Hedwiga Reicher, who had a house in Carmel.

> She was less than successful on the stage, being too tall, and tragic in the old-fashioned manner; but when she stood up in our little room under the low ceiling and recited a tragic ballad—"Edward, Edward"—for a few

people gathered there, the experience made me want to build a heroic poem to match her formidable voice and rather colossal beauty. I thought these would be absurdly out of place in any contemporary story, so I looked back toward the feet of Aeschylus, and cast this woman for the part of Cassandra in my poem.[39]

Already here we have a clue to Jeffers's treatment of the material: he identifies with the stately Cassandra, whom he contrasts with his "low-statured" Clytemnestra, "sinewed with strength" (1:119). Elsewhere Jeffers voiced his sympathy with the Trojan princess whose prophecies no one heeds: for instance, in the poem "Cassandra" (in *The Double Axe*, 1948) he adjures her to be wise and cease her efforts. "No: you'll still mumble in a corner a crust of truth, to men / And gods disgusting.—You and I, Cassandra" (3:121).[40] In order to keep her longer on the stage, he contrives to have her killed, not by Clytemnestra in the early part of the play but much later by Orestes himself.

The work amounts to Jeffers's effort to rewrite Aeschylus's *Oresteia* (or, at least, its first two parts) for modern times. Originally called "The New Oresteia" and "The Last Oresteia," it went through a third version entitled "Beyond Tragedy" before the tower emerged as the dominating image.[41] The verse drama, which is divided into three parts and interspersed with narrative passages, begins with the action of *Agamemnon*: the king's return from Troy and his murder in the bath by his wife, Clytemnestra, to avenge his sacrifice of their daughter Iphigenia; and her seizure of power in the city-state of Mycenae. Part 2 opens eight years later with a bleak vision of the future pronounced by Cassandra before the traditional action of the *Electra* takes place: following vacillations and egged on by his sister, Orestes strikes down Clytemnestra and, in a moment of confusion, stabs Cassandra as well. In the conclusion, which has no counterpart in the Greek sources, Electra seeks to persuade Orestes to assume the throne of Mycenae where, she suggests, they will rule in an incestuous union and he will be freed from the blood-curse of Clytemnestra's murder. But Orestes rejects her offer and leaves the city to seek his freedom in another way: not by the traditional legal dispensation but by transcending humankind altogether.[42]

The work is basically a study of power—the lust for, and abuse of, power that Jeffers regarded as the single greatest factor alienating humankind from its place in the natural world.[43] The high point of part 1 is the scene in which Clytemnestra, having slain Agamemnon, emerges from the palace to confront the people of Mycenae, while the spirit of her dead husband exhorts the populace through the mouth of Cassandra. Because Aegisthus has not yet arrived with his troops, she must control the people through the sheer force of her will: first through her mesmerizing gaze and then by exposing her body to public view, dominating the men of Mycenae by a display of sheer naked power, political as well as sexual. She succeeds in working her will and seizing power; but in the meantime her children, Orestes and Electra, have escaped her vengeance. In the transition bridging parts 1 and 2 Cassandra, who has already "seen Egypt and Nineveh / Crumble" (1:147), foretells in a compelling vision the ravages wrought by the continuing struggle for power on nations and empires of the future down to the moment "When America has eaten Europe and takes tribute of Asia" (1:148). Orestes and Electra return to wreak their legendary vengeance upon Clytemnestra and Aegisthus. (In a kind of trance Orestes also kills Cassandra.) But in part 3 Orestes refuses to play out his role by assuming the political power he has earned by killing his mother and her lover, and which is urged upon him by Electra, who turns out to be her mother's true daughter in her power-crazed ambition.

The idea of power preoccupies Orestes as well, but in a radically distorted manner: in his mind it is weirdly identified with incest. The words in which he deliberates the execution of Clytemnestra are unmistakably sexual in their ambivalence.

> Dip in my sword
> Into my fountain? Did I truly, little and helpless,
> Lie in the arms, feed on the breast there?
>
> (1:161)

As he vacillates, he wonders if he should "Dip my wand into my fountain" (1:162) or "enter his fountain" (1:163). Following his slaying of Clytemnestra and Cassandra, whom in his confusion he also takes to be his mother, Orestes rushes out into the countryside. The next day he relates to Electra a dream in which precisely the same image returns, again in an incestuous context: "I thought I embraced you / More than brotherwise . . . possessed, you call it . . . entered the fountain" (1:169). Electra tells him that he must now assume power in Mycenae and that she will help him to exorcise the ghost of Clytemnestra "with my life, or with my body" (1:171)—that is, by dying or by yielding to him sexually:

What you want you shall have:
And rule in Mycenae. Nothing, nothing is denied
   you. If I knew which of the two choices
Would quiet you, I would do and not speak, not ask
   you.

As a maiden, still untouched by any man, she would find
it difficult to offer up her virtue; but death would be easy:
"if fear of desire / Drives you away: it is easy for me not
to be." Orestes has already made his decision to forgo the
incestuous invitation to power and absolution offered by
Electra. Incest plays a conspicuous role in Jeffers's work
of this period, accounting in large measure for the shock
value of *Tamar* (1924)—the story of a child of incest who
commits incest with her brother, tempts her father to the
point of incest, and then manages to destroy her whole
incestuous family in a great conflagration. Jeffers was obsessed with incest not for sexual reasons but as an image
of the human impulse to what he called the "excess of
introversion" that has hampered and distorted natural
human development, as he explained in a letter to his
friend and supporter George Sterling.[44]

The incest theme—you are right of course. I never had
a sister, and here is what inexperience does to one! I
think of two reasons why it occurs to me; first because
it breaks taboo more violently than the other irregular-
ities and so *may* be of a more tragic nature; and more
important, it seems to symbolize human turned-in-
wardness, the perpetual struggle to get ahead of each
other, help or hinder each other, love each other, scare
each other, subdue or exalt each other, that absorbs 99
per cent of human energy. For instance the man who
discovers a mountain isn't happy until he collects

other men to admire it, or until he fights other men for possession of it. This excess of introversion is a sort of racial incest, or so I imagine, but we'd better find another symbol.

The temptation to power, in sum, is symbolized by the incestuous thoughts that obsess Orestes unconsciously when he murders his mother, and consciously as he considers his future as a ruler, with his sister Electra, of Mycenae. On Jeffers's psychic scale, then, Clytemnestra and Electra represent the pure desire for power. Cassandra is the prophetess who understands the ravages of absolute power, but who is utterly powerless herself to do anything about it. And Orestes is that rare individual who succeeds in liberating himself from the all-too-human lust for power.

For during the night in the wilderness he has had a mystical vision in which he leaves human history behind to be reunited with nature: "I entered the life of the brown forest / And the great life of the ancient peaks, the patience of stone" (1:176–77). In sum, his mystical vision has revealed to Orestes another road to freedom: casting off his humanity and rejoining the impersonal forces of pure nature. In 1929 Jeffers sought to explain his meaning by referring to "moments of visionary enlightenment."[45] "Almost the whole of human energy is expended inward, on itself, in loving, hating, governing, cajoling, amusing, its own members"—in short, on what Jeffers calls incest. "We can't turn back the civilization, not at least until it collapses, and our descendents will have to develop a new sort of nature—will have to 'break out of humanity'—or suffer considerably—probably both."

The central theme of the work—the destructive human struggle for power in contrast to the timeless peace of nature—is underscored by the imagery, in which the permanence of stone plays the most important role. The word "stone" occurs five times in the scenic directions of the first page alone (1:119), establishing the mood for the coming scenes. Helen of Troy is "the beautiful sea-flower / Cut in clear stone." The powerful, crafty Clytemnestra stands on the "great steps of stone above the steep street"; when she raises her arms, her soldiers' spear-butts "thundered on the stone," while the queen, "setting the golden-sandaled feet carefully, stone by stone," descended to meet her king. As Robert J. Brophy has observed, rock symbolizes for Clytemnestra "the solidity of civilization, the building-blocks for cities, the permanence and justice upholding the Mycenean acropolis."[46] She calls human society, which tolerates any crime, "the stone garden of the plants that pass nature" (1:144). Agamemnon, in turn, "expects the stones of the Acropolis to speak out against the crime which subverts the city; he invokes the stone towers to fall upon the woman who outrages justice and the gods."

Between parts 2 and 3 it is the stones of the porch and the great stairway of Mycenae, scoured of the blood that had defiled them, which speak and provide the transition. "The world is younger than we are," begins one of the great stones. Another says that humankind, "noisy and very mobile creatures," will disappear in time. "What creatures?" asks yet another. "The active ones, that have two ends let downward, / A mongrel race, mixed of soft stone with fugitive water" (1:166).

Cassandra, for her part, recognizes the futility of any

faith in human power or the towers erected by mere human ambition. In a grand apocalyptic vision she exclaims:

> If anywhere in the world
> Were a tower with foundations, or a treasure-
>   chamber
> With a firm vault, or a walled fortress
> That stood on the years, not staggering, not moving
> As the mortar were mixed with wine for water
> And poppy for lime: they reel, they are all
>   drunkards,
> The piled strengths of the world: no pyramid
> In bitter Egypt in the desert
> But skips at moonrise; . . .
> . . . I am sick after steadfastness
> Watching the world cataractlike
> Pour screaming onto steep ruins. . . .   (1:144)

It is appropriate, therefore, that Orestes, when he renounces earthly ambition and human history, feels himself at one with that stable geological world: "it is I that am like stone walking" (1:178). As Electra turns away in disappointment, Orestes strides into the clear dawn. Legend will report that he died of a serpent-bite. But life and death mean nothing "To him who had climbed the tower beyond time, consciously, / and cast humanity, entered the earlier fountain" (1:178).

The work ends with this invocation of the "tower beyond time"—that is, the mythical ideal of a timeless state of detachment that may be achieved by those who have endured tragedy and thus passed beyond it. Jeffers explained his intention to George Sterling: "My idea was to present as a part of the action, the culminating part, that liberation which the witness is supposed to feel—to let one of the agonists be freed, as the audience is expected to be, from passion and the other birth-marks of humanity. Therefore, *beyond* tragedy—tragedy and what results."[47] In a subsequent letter to Mark Van Doren he wrote, "the 'Tower beyond Tragedy'—romantic title—meant the state of a mystic to whom tragedy was impossible because he had escaped finally from the sense of his own—not important exactly—separateness."[48]

◘ 6 ◘

In the following years Jeffers refined his philosophical attitude, which he came to call Inhumanism, "a shifting of emphasis and significance from man to not-man," as he put it in his preface to *The Double Axe* (1948).[49] "This manner of thought and feeling is neither misanthropic nor pessimist. . . . It offers a reasonable detachment as rule of conduct, instead of love, hate and envy. It neutralizes fanaticism and wild hopes; but it provides magnificence for the religious instinct, and satisfies our need to admire greatness and rejoice in beauty." It is human consciousness—the lust for knowledge, power, glory—that has deprived man of joy and strength. "I tell you unconsciousness is the treasure, the tower, the fortress" (1:395) was his message "To a Young Artist" (in *Cawdor*, 1928).

If Orestes had to leave his sister and his city in order to find his symbolic tower beyond tragedy (or time), Jeffers had completed a real stone tower that was for the next three decades to afford him precisely the kind of refuge from modernity that he sought. In good weather he liked to write in the tower, and he often contemplated

Fig. 15. Robinson Jeffers at Hawk Tower, 1925.
Photographer, Lewis Josselyn. Permission of
Robinson Jeffers Tor House Foundation.

his verses on its battlements. This is not to say that the
traditional image of the proud tower, invoked by Cassandra, does not appear again in Jeffers's poetry. As he
watched the approach of World War II from his tower,
Jeffers observed in "Night without Sleep" (in *Such Coun-
sels You Gave Me*, 1937) that "The greatest civilization that
has ever existed builds / itself higher towers on breaking
foundations" (2:558). Generally, however, the tower
shows up as an image for that permanence and stability
that he recognizes in nature. Toward the end of his life,

after his wife's death, he seems to have clung even more fervently to the permanence of the tower. Imagining (in "Star-Swirls," from *The Beginning and the End*, 1963) the destruction of civilization following the melting of the polar ice caps, Jeffers assumes that even his seaside cliff will be flooded. But his tower, whose thick walls he built with Portland cement and granite, "will hold against the sea's buffeting, it will become / Geological, fossil and permanent" (3:476). Another poem from the same period imagines that not natural disaster but population explosion will push in and destroy the woods he planted and his stonework.

> Only the little tower,
> Four-foot-thick-walled and useless may stand for
>   a time.
> That and some verses. It is curious that flower-
>   soft verse
> Is sometimes harder than granite, tougher than a
>   steel cable, more alive than life.   (3:477)

(Again we recognize the Horatian theme of the monument that is *aere perennius*.) The late poems revolve almost obsessively around his stone complex.

> There is a jaggle of masonry here, on a small hill
> Above the gray-mouthed Pacific, cottages and a
>   thick-walled tower, all made of rough sea-rock
> And Portland cement.   (3:465)

The poet goes on to imagine that, fifty years hence, his ghost will return to inspect the site. When the new owner comes suspiciously to the door, the ghost explains that he is simply looking at the walls he once built—and dismayed at the devastation of the trees he once planted.

Shortly after its completion, and at the zenith of his own fame and popularity (in "Soliloquy" from *The Women at Point Sur*, 1927), Jeffers predicted that his views would in time come to be called "heartless and blind," and visualized himself "in gray old years in the evening leaning / Over the gray stones of the tower-top." But the poet, "laired in the rock" and as indifferent to human-kind as the tower itself, "sheds pleasure and pain like hail-stones" (1:215). Hawk Tower became for Jeffers the sym-bolic "tower beyond tragedy" that he sought out for his own communion with nature:

> On the small marble-paved platform
> On the turret on the head of the tower,
> Watching the night deepen.
> I feel the rock-edge of the continent
> Reel eastward with me below the broad stars.
> I lean on the broad worn stones of the parapet top
> And the stones and my hands that touch them reel
>   eastward.   (2:160)

Here in "Margrave" (in *Thurso's Landing*, 1932) the tower is the timeless vantage point from which the poet con-templates the tragedy produced by the consciousness that has alienated man from "The sane uninfected far-outer universes" (2:161). Following his account of the murder committed by Walter Margrave, which is the principal topic of the narrative poem, the poet finds himself once again on his tower:

> On the little stone-girded platform
> Over the earth and the ocean
> I seem to have stood a long time and watched the
>   stars pass.

They also shall perish I believe.
Here to-day, gone to-morrow, desperate wee
    galaxies
Scattering themselves and shining their substance
    away
Like a passionate thought. It is very well ordered.

(2:171)

For Jeffers, then, the tower that he built for his wife in imitation of Yeats's tower at Ballylee provided the real and symbolic refuge from which, with Horatian irony and the Lucretian detachment that he called Inhumanism, he contemplated what he regarded as the inevitable disintegration of civilization and the reassuring timelessless of the natural world.

CHAPTER FOUR

Rainer Maria Rilke: The Tower of Desire

Fig. 16. Château de Muzot, ca. 1920. Courtesy of Insel Verlag, Frankfurt am Main.

1

Towers constitute one of the most prominent images in Rilke's oeuvre, occurring almost a hundred times in poems alone composed over a period of some thirty years.[1] This is hardly surprising in view of the fact that Rilke (1875–1926) was born and raised in Prague—"this rich, gigantic epic of architecture,"[2] as he called it, fabled for the towers and spires on its churches, bridges, and castle. "The gabled, towery city is oddly built," begins Rilke's essay on the "Prague Artist" Emil Orlik (1900). "Watchful towers speak of every hour, and at night their lonely voices meet one another" (5:469). Prague art, he continues, can be understood only in the context of a childhood spent in these surroundings. The same applies a fortiori to Prague writers.

Rilke's early volume of verse, a celebration of Prague entitled *Offerings to the Lares* (*Larenopfer*, 1895),[3] contains many allusions to the hometown towers. The opening poem, "In the Old House" ("Im alten Haus") finds the poet contemplating the city from his window: most of the buildings are blurred in the dusk; "only the verdigris-green tower-cupola of Saint Nicholas's rises clear before my eyes" (1:9). The next poem mentions "lofty towers full of ringing" (1:9); and a tribute to Prague's castle ("Der Hradschin") imagines that the more recent towers of the city peer up at the bulb on St. Veit's Tower like a group of children looking up at their father (1:11). Several other poems locate the poet, as in the first one, gazing out of his window at night while the moonlight twines itself in silver strands around the black bulb of a church tower ("das Mondlicht windet silbersträhnig / sich um den schwarzen Kirchturmknauf"; "Vigilien II," 1:48), and where he sees towers domed like acorns or pointed like slender pears ("Vom Lugaus," 1:13). In his "Two Prague Tales" (1899) familiar towers are indicated from time to time as landmarks or for local color. In these early works, however, the poet is simply sharpening his powers of description; the image remains conventional, often serving as little more than a poetic Baedeker to the towers that dominate the city.

Some of the early poems also incorporate familiar folktale motifs. One, entitled simply "Ghost Tower" ("Gespensterturm," 1894), depicts an old tower that is rumored to be haunted; decent folk avoid it even by day, but it is sometimes occupied by itinerant rabble (3:115). The "Maidens' Songs" of 1898 invoke the ancient motif of the sequestration of maidens: "We always live deep within the tower" (1:178). In another context, the poet's soul wears a maiden's dress and has silken hair: she lives far away behind many walls, as though in a tower and not yet liberated by the poet ("wohnt wie im Turm, noch nicht von mir befreit").[4] In other cities as well, towers continue to catch the eye of this Prague-born poet as a focal point around which all else revolves. On his trip to Florence in 1897 Rilke observed from the rooftop of his hotel how "the towers seem to climb up more slenderly from the wave of the cupolas."[5]

In many of the early examples the tower is associated with the sound of its bells. "The tower calls out the noon in its accustomed pose" ("Der Narr," 3:131). "In the evening a tower stands alone with its bells and is silent" ("Im Abend steht ein Turm allein," 3:741). This motif is transferred to the poet in one of the love poems to Lou

Andreas-Salomé ("Dir zur Feier," 1898), where the poet speaks of her preference for quiet, which clothes her like silk, while the storms of life transform him into a tower:

> Wir lieben Stille und Sturm,
> die bauen und bilden uns beide:
> Dich—kleidet die Stille wie Seide,
> mich—machen die Stürme zum Turm. . . (3:182)

□ 2 □

Rilke's trips to Russia, in 1899 and again in 1900, lent a pronounced religious aspect to the earlier romantic image. From the very beginning vague religious associations were attached to the towers. In 1897 we catch an allusion to the church bells in Venice, which are personified as singing worshipers ("AVE weht von den Türmen her," 1:118). But in Russia, and especially in Holy Moscow, Rilke was obsessed by the religious life and culture that unfolded beneath the towers and spires of the Kremlin and other churches. In one of his first letters he wrote, "My voice has gotten lost amidst the Kremlin bells, and my eye, after the golden radiance of the cupolas, sees nothing more."[6] Three years later Rilke recalled the impact made upon him when, arriving on Maundy Thursday, he participated in the Easter ceremonies in Moscow.

I don't have words enough to tell you what an experience it was for me to see Moscow; my whole childhood, which, flooded over by the years of a fearful and confused youth, had been lost to me, emerged again like a sunken city, and when I stood on Easter night with my small candle in the Kremlin, the bell on "Ivan Velikij" tolled so powerfully and mightily that I be-

lieved I was hearing the heartbeat of a land waiting
from day to day upon its future.[7]

In the magnificent poetic record of those Russian impres-
sions, *The Book of Hours* (*Das Stunden-Buch*, 1899, 1901,
1903) the tower emerges explicitly as an image for God. In
the opening poem the poet-monk is awakened by the
metallic ringing of the hour that falls from the bell tower.
The monk lives his life, he tells us, in a gyre spiraling
around a center. Circling for millennia around God, the
ancient tower, he still does not know whether he is a
falcon, a storm, or a mighty song.

> Ich kreise um Gott, um den uralten Turm,
> und ich kreise jahrtausendelang;
> und ich weiß noch nicht: bin ich ein Falke,
>   ein Sturm
> oder ein großer Gesang.   (1:253)

God, it turns out, is a cathedrallike project that mankind
constructs, atom by atom:

> Wir bauen an dir mit zitternden Händen
> und wir türmen Atom auf Atom.
> Aber wer kann dich vollenden,
> du Dom.   (1:261)

> (We build at you with trembling hands / and we
> heap atom upon atom. / But who can complete
> you, / cathedral?)

But in a passage that strikingly anticipates Eliot's *The
Waste Land*, the poet-monk remarks that the great cities
of the world fall apart and are destroyed before God's
towers can be crowned with their cupolas, and before his
radiant brow can arise from miles of mosaic:

Was ist Rom?
Es zerfällt.
Was ist die Welt?
Sie wird zerschlagen
eh deine Türme Kuppeln tragen,
eh aus Meilen von Mosaik
deine strahlende Stirne stieg.   (1:261–62)

(What is Rome? / It falls apart. / What is the world?
/ It is shattered / before your towers bear their cupolas, / before from miles of mosaic / your radiant
brow arose.)

And in an early draft omitted from the final version of
The Book of Hours the monk apostrophizes his fellow
monks who have not yet been redeemed: one day they
will stand like brides to greet him, their Lord who stands
before their veils "like a tower of amethyst" (3:347).

These religious associations can be traced through
many later poems. In "Sankt Georg" (1907), for instance,
the maiden's prayer is said to stand alongside "as towers
stand" (1:618), while the knight battles with the dragon.
In a poem written around 1914 ("Wie der Abendwind")
the tower is invoked metaphorically to characterize the
steadfastness of an angel who "stands like a tower beside
the sea" (2:78).

◘ 3 ◘

Rilke's appreciation of towers was expanded beyond the
touristic and folkloristic by his contact with Rodin,
whom he first visited in 1902 with the commission to
write a monograph about the famous sculptor (and one-

Fig. 17. Auguste Rodin, *La Tour du Travail*
(1898). Permission of Musée Rodin, Paris.

time teacher of Rilke's wife, Clara Westhoff). Thanks to
Rodin, whom he addressed as "Cher Maître," he began
to understand the architectural function of towers and to
sense as well their symbolic potentialities. On a trip to
Chartres in 1906, undertaken in Rodin's company, he
wrote an enthusiastic letter describing his impression of
the cathedral and employing botanical imagery to suggest
the sensation of pure verticality and upward-striving mo-
tion aroused by the two towers: "above a mass of small,
cramped houses we saw one tower rise from the crush,
which blossomed at the top with Gothic, and another
beside it like a Gothic bud."[8] The following year Rilke

wrote the second part of his monograph on Rodin (1907), in which he devoted several pages to the sculptor's model for a *Tour du Travail*, whose spiral staircase displays a conspicuous resemblance to sixteenth-century representations of the Tower of Babel.

> On a rectangular, rather spacious base rises a round tower. Its open arcades suggest at first the Pisan campanile; but the arches here stand one on top of the other and arranged in stories; they wind upward in a spiral band, where the belt of a three-dimensional cornice holds them together. The conclusion of the whole is formed by a group of two winged figures, who rest upon the platform enclosed by the cornice. (5:243–44)

Rilke goes on to describe the figures of artisans that will decorate the crypt in the base. "From here one enters the tower. It consists of a massive column around which, in a gentle incline, the spiral staircase leads. It is separated from outside by the arcades through which abundant light falls on the reliefs on the opposite wall. These, animating the surface of the column, accompany the staircase all the way to the top." The tower as a whole exemplifies the history of work from its primitive beginnings to its most sophisticated modern forms.

It was this new awareness that, in early July 1906, inspired the poem "Die Kathedrale," a synthetic image that owes more to Nôtre Dame in Paris than to Chartres. The *Dinggedichte* ("thing-poems") that characterize Rilke's *Neue Gedichte* (1907) no longer restrict themselves to incidental reference or passing descriptions but seek to render the essence of the object described. Rilke described how he learned to see and create from Rodin: the object of art must be even more determined than reality itself:

"removed from all contingency, transported out of all unclarity, lifted out of time and handed over to space, it has become lasting, capable of eternity."[9] This effort to imitate the *modelé* that Rilke admired in Rodin's sculptures also incorporates the genesis of the object, not unlike the manner in which Rodin's sculptures often show how they emerge from the stone from which they are hewn. The conclusion of "Die Kathedrale" makes use, to be sure, of the conventional association of towers and tolling bells; but it also introduces for the first time the ominous presence of death, which emerged as a powerful theme, even obsession, in the works of these years: notably in the lyrical novel *The Notebooks of Malte Laurids Brigge* (1910). Rilke suggests now that, along with bells, death resides in the towers which, full of renunciation (that is, uncapped by spires), stop climbing.

> Das Leben zögerte im Stundenschlagen,
> und in den Türmen, welche voll Entsagen
> auf einmal nicht mehr stiegen, war der Tod.
>
> (1:498)

> (Life hesitated in the tolling of the hours, / and in the towers which, full of renunciation, / suddenly no longer rose, was death.)

�« 4 »◌

In 1906, shortly after finishing "Die Kathedrale" and his other so-called cathedral poems, Rilke spent three weeks in Belgium, traveling by way of Ieper (Ypres) and Veurne to the coastal spas and returning to Paris by way of Brugge (Bruges) and Ghent. The account that he wrote

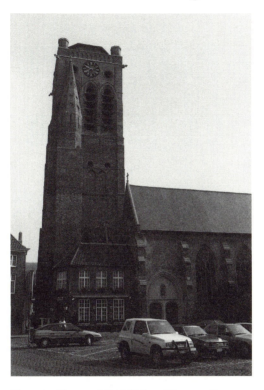

Fig. 18. Tower of St.-Niklaas, Veurne. Courtesy
of Dienst voor Toerisme, Veurne.

a year later focuses, surprisingly, not on the two better-
known cities but on Veurne ("Furnes," 1907). The essay
opens with two pages on Brugge, known as "the dead
city" ever since Georges Rodenbach's popular novel
Bruges-la-morte (1892), and singles out its famous towers:
notably the Beffroi, which climbs story by story to scatter
its carillon sounds somewhere above (6:1005). Rilke goes
on to suggest that travelers are better prepared to appreciate Brugge and its noted towers if they have already experienced in Veurne the "excessiveness" (*Maßlosigkeit*) of
Flemish towers, which "rise above the gables as though

they belonged in heaven" (6:1007–8). Following a description of the "enormous square" Rilke mentions the church portals of St.-Niklaas's, which lies "half submerged, as though forced down into the earth by the pressure of the flat-topped tower." In the final paragraph the poet recalls the bell-ringer who only two months earlier (Rilke mistakenly assumed that the accident took place the day before his arrival) had plunged to his death while toiling with the great bell in the rafters of the tower, "half dancing and half embattled, alone with it above the dark abyss of the tower and swallowed by the storm of its voice" (6:1015–16).[10] (Even in his prose Rilke cannot escape the rhyming association of "Turm" with "Sturm," which has recurred almost formulaically in his poems for over ten years.)

The impression of pressing weight, the image of abyss, and the association of death dominate the poem "The Tower," which he wrote around the same time (18 July 1907), and which goes far beyond the conventional associations of the early poems.

Der Turm

Tour St.-Nicolas, Furnes

ERD-INNERES. Als wäre dort, wohin
du blindlings steigst, erst Erdenoberfläche,
zu der du steigst im schrägen Bett der Bäche,
die langsam aus dem suchenden Gerinn

der Dunkelheit entsprungen sind, durch die
sich dein Gesicht, wie auferstehend, drängt
und die du plötzlich *siehst*, als fiele sie
aus diesem Abgrund, der dich überhängt

und den du, wie er riesig über dir
sich umstürzt in dem dämmernden Gestühle,

erkennst, erschreckt und fürchtend, im Gefühle:
o wenn er steigt, behangen wie ein Stier—:

Da aber nimmt dich aus der engen Endung
windiges Licht. Fast fliegend siehst du hier
die Himmel wieder, Blendung über Blendung,
und dort die Tiefen, wach und voll Verwendung,

und kleine Tage wie bei Patenier,
gleichzeitige, mit Stunde neben Stunde,
durch die die Brücken springen wie die Hunde,
dem hellen Wege immer auf der Spur,

den unbeholfne Häuser manchmal nur
verbergen, bis er ganz im Hintergrunde
beruhigt geht durch Buschwerk und Natur.

(1:532–33)

(EARTH-INTERIOR. As though there, whither
you blindly climb, were the earth's surface,
toward which you ascend in the slanted bed of the
  streams
that have emerged slowly, from the searching flow

of the darkness through which
your sight, as though resurrected, penetrates
and which you suddenly *see*, as though it were
  falling
out of this abyss that is suspended above you

and which, as it hugely collapses above you
in the lightening belfry,
you recognize, startled and afraid, in the feeling:
o, if it rises, adorned like a steer—:

But then out of the narrow ending
windy light seizes you. Almost flying you see here
the skies again, brilliance over brilliance,
and there the depths, alert and full of usefulness,

and small days as in Patenier,
simultaneous ones, with hour beside hour,
through which the bridges leap like dogs,
ever on the trail of the bright path,

which clumsy houses sometimes only
obscure, until far in the background
it passes calmly through shrubs and nature.)

Following the first word—"EARTH-INTERIOR."—a
single sentence—actually the protasis of an unusually
complex sentence, consisting of a dozen incapsulated
clauses and extending over three quatrains—describes the
climb up the narrow spiral staircase of the tower to the
battlements above as though—the typical Rilkean inversion introduced by "als wäre"—it were a blind ascent
from below ground up to the surface of the earth, like
that of springs of water seeking the surface from their
sluggish sources. No longer taking a stance outside or on
top of the tower, as in the essay and most earlier poems,
the poet leads us into the dark and claustrophobigenic
stairwell, which at Veurne is located in a narrow windowless annex attached to the external wall of the tower.
In his essay Rilke speaks of the tower's abyss as it might
appear to someone—a tourist or, indeed, the unlucky
bell-ringer himself—looking down from the belfry. In
the poem, in contrast, he imagines that he is peering up
from below at the impenetrable darkness of the same
abyss, like subterranean springs struggling toward the
light. As he approaches the top of the annex, he suddenly
becomes aware of the thinning darkness, which is said
to overhang the poet and fall down upon him as he
struggles up the windowless staircase. When the poet
steps out into the gloom of the belfry, he is suddenly

overcome by terror at the abyss, which had only a short time before killed its denizen and which is therefore said to threaten the intruder like a steer laden (with a bell around its neck).[11] Following the colon, the apodosis of the same sustained sentence leads the viewer (in much simpler clauses and phrases that have an emancipating effect after the complexities of the protasis) out of the dark stairwell and murky belfry up onto the battlement of the tower (which at Veurne has no spire), where he can see both the blinding light of the sky and the cultivated landscape below, which is divided by the interstices of the parapet into small segments resembling landscapes by Patenier (whose vistas are almost invariably seen from a height) and held together by bridges indicating the sometimes hidden course of the canals that lead the eye past the town into the landscape beyond. The poem, whose syntax—moving from complexity to a liberating simplicity—exemplifies its meaning, succeeds in suggesting not only that the ascent of the tower is also a gyrelike ascent of consciousness from an ominous darkness to blinding illumination, but also that achieved consciousness enables the poet to structure the reality surrounding him in the form of art.[12]

◻ 5 ◻

The image of the tower as a metaphor of human existence and its grief shows up elsewhere after this key poem. A fragmentary poem from the summer of 1907, "The Lonely One" ("Der Einsame") begins with the drastic image[13] of a tower growing out of the poet's heart, on whose edge he is precariously placed, looking out over nothing but pain and ineffability and world:

> Nein, ein Turm soll sein aus meinem Herzen
> und ich selbst an seinen Rand gestellt;
> wo sonst nichts mehr ist noch einmal Schmerzen
> und Unsäglichkeit, noch einmal Welt.   (2:349)

"Christ's Descent into Hell" ("Christi Höllenfahrt," 1913) ends with a striking genitive metaphor in which the savior steps out onto the tower of his sufferance ("Turm seines Duldens"), where he stands without breath, without railing, "the proprietor of pains" ("Eigentümer der Schmerzen," 2:58). A letter of 1915 contains a passage that strikingly anticipates the concept of the "objective correlative" that T. S. Eliot was soon to elaborate in his critical essays. Recalling the landscapes of Spain, Rilke writes that in Toledo "the external object itself—tower, mountain, bridge—possessed simultaneously the incredible, incomparable intensity of the inner equivalents through which one would have wished to represent it. Appearance and vision came together, as it were, in the object itself."[14] Another letter of 1915, finally, develops a remarkable image catalyzed by reflections on Tolstoy (whom Rilke had met on his two trips to Russia). Observing that Tolstoy analyzed many varieties of the fear of death ("Todesangst"), Rilke goes on to conjecture—in a vision worthy of Piranesi—that Tolstoy's relationship to death must have been "a sublimely permeated fear, a fugue of fear as it were, a gigantic structure, a tower of anxiety with passages and staircases and railingless ledges and precipices in every direction."[15]

Such interiorizations of the tower, which in his earlier works had been initially a conventional external point of orientation and then gradually a symbol for the poet's own consciousness, mark the process exemplified in the poem "Wendung" (1914), in which Rilke describes his progress in the art of *seeing* ("Anschaun"), which he had begun under Rodin's tutelage (and which constitutes one of the principal themes of his novel *Malte Laurids Brigge*).[16] He has become such a virtuoso in the act of pure contemplation that the external world now enters his vision without resistance, like the towers startled to find themselves reconstructed suddenly in his inner eye:

> Türme schaute er so,
> daß sie erschraken:
> wieder sie bauend, hinan, plötzlich, in Einem!
>
> (2:82)

But now that he has learned how to *see*, the envisioned world must be permeated by love in order to thrive because there are limits to what is accessible to sight alone: the work of sight must give way to the work of the heart on the images within:

> Denn des Anschauns, siehe, ist eine Grenze.
> Und die geschautere Welt
> will in der Liebe gedeihn.
>
> Werk des Gesichts ist getan,
> tue nun Herz-Werk
> an den Bildern in dir. . . . (2:83–84)

(For, behold, there is a boundary to seeing. / And the more intensively seen world / wishes to thrive in love.

Work of seeing is done, / now do heart-work / on the images within yourself.)

A similar thought is elaborated more extensively in one of the seven (untitled) phallocentric poems that Rilke wrote in Munich in late 1915.[17] In a vision with conspicuously erotic overtones he tells the woman apostrophized in the first word ("Schwindende" = "fading" or "waning") that she has still not truly known what a tower is.[18] But now she shall apprehend a tower through the power of internalization. And once she has erected that tower in her imagination (and with the more sexual implication: within herself) and it has arisen before her, the poet will take possession of its cozy space, step out onto its dome, and fire off rockets of feeling:

> Schwindende, du kennst die Türme nicht.
> Doch nun sollst du einen Turm gewahren
> mit dem wunderbaren
> Raum in dir. Verschließ dein Angesicht.
> Aufgerichtet hast du ihn
> ahnungslos mit Blick und Wink und Wendung.
> Plötzlich starrt er von Vollendung,
> und ich, Seliger, darf ihn beziehn.
> Ach wie bin ich eng darin.
> Schmeichle mir, zur Kuppel auszutreten:
> um in deine weichen Nächte hin
> mit dem Schwung schooßblendender Raketen
> mehr Gefühl zu schleudern, als ich bin.

(2:436–37)

(Waning one, you don't know towers. / But now you shall become aware of a tower / with the wonderful /space within yourself. Close your countenance. / You have erected it / unsuspectingly with look and gesture and move. / Suddenly it is rigid with fulfillment, / and I, blissful, may enter it. / Ah,

how snug I am in there. / Coax me to step out onto
the dome: / in order to hurl into your gentle nights
/ with the verve of womb-dazzling rockets / more
feeling than I am.)

It would be difficult to imagine a more powerfully erotic
image than the tower in this poem, which is made erect
by the attraction of the beloved, which becomes rigid as
the poet, blissful, fires off his "womb-dazzling rockets."

◲ 6 ◲

Given this complex attitude toward towers, which com-
bines introspection with sexuality, reverence for the divine with the mad architectonics of *Angst*, it is no wonder
that Rilke was moved by an ambivalent mixture of emotions when he had the opportunity to live in a tower of
his own. From time to time in the past, in the course of
his peregrinations among his wealthy and often noble
friends and patrons, the poet had already inhabited a few
towers. Rilke spent the summer of 1904 in Sweden, at the
estate of the painter Ernst Norlind and his fiancée Hanna
Larsson at Borgeby-gard. The "castle" was actually an ancient fortress tower around which, as Rilke described it in
a letter to his wife, more modest living quarters had been
annexed, with the residential section to the left of the
tower.[19] In the winter of 1910 his publisher, Anton Kippenberg, urging him to finish his novel *Malte Laurids
Brigge*, invited Rilke to spend several weeks at his estate
in Leipzig, where the poet had at his disposal the "tower
room" attached to the Kippenbergs' mansion—bright,
sunny, and just right for a poet, he assured Rilke.[20] The

following year, from October 1911 until May 1912, Rilke was a guest of Princess Marie von Thurn und Taxis at Castle Duino, an ancient fortress high on a cliff overlooking the Adriatic near Trieste— "this castle, towering up immensely beside the sea, like a promontory of human existence"[21]—where he wrote the first two of his *Duino Elegies*. And in 1916 Rilke spent two days at Burghausen, due east of Munich on the Austrian border, where the writer Regina Ullmann was living with her mother in one of the turreted residential towers typical of the region. (Ullmann's own poems contain no references to her tower.) Rilke inquired about rents for the towers and, sending a picture postcard to Princess Marie, wrote that he dreamed of "establishing a little refuge for myself in one of the towers with a few pieces of furniture."[22]

Ten years after beginning the elegies at Duino, the poet was to finish them in a tower of his own. Rilke, who initially responded to the outbreak of World War I with the enthusiasm that characterized many of his generation, rapidly changed his views. He fought desperately to avoid military service, which was finally reduced to six months of light archival work in Vienna, and his views became increasingly pacifistic. By the end of the war, back in Munich, he became sympathetic to the teachings of such leftwing revolutionaries as Kurt Eisner and Ernst Toller and was harassed by the police. In the summer of 1919, hoping to get away at least for a time from the political and social turmoil of postwar Germany, he went to Switzerland on a lecture tour, which stretched into a year as the poet found still intact in the neutral country the *bildungs-bürgerlich* culture and wealthy benefactors that he required for his support. At the end of that year, in August 1920, he met the painter Baladine Klossowska and, with

the impulsiveness that typified most of his many love af-
fairs, decided to remain near her in Switzerland. Always
suspicious of those ties that bind, and dependent as he
was upon the kindness of strangers, Rilke did not stay in
Geneva, where Merline (the nickname by which he came
to call her) lived with her two sons, but spent the winter
near Zurich at the château of other wealthy benefactors.
However, during the euphoric first weeks of his affair
with Merline, he had made his first trip to Sion and Sierre
in the Valais, where Merline's estranged husband was
staying. Rilke was immediately taken by the landscape of
the southern Swiss canton, which reminded him, as he
often remarked, of Spain and Provence. Accordingly,
when his months at Château Berg were terminated, and
he was casting about once again for a more permanent
residence and, above all, for a place where he could finally
complete the elegies begun nine years earlier at Duino, he
thought immediately of the Valais and enlisted Merline's
assistance in finding an appropriate place.

On 28 June 1921, they arrived in Sierre and, the next
day, visited a realtor, who himself lived in "La Tour
Goubin," one of the residential towers, called "castles"
locally, that dot the mountainsides of the Valais. Rilke
was delighted with the tower but dismayed by the two
utterly unsuitable properties that were shown to him. On
30 June, on the point of leaving Sierre in disappointment, Rilke and his companion noticed in a hairdresser's
shopwindow the photograph of a tower *du treisième siècle*
with the indication that it was for rent or sale.[23] The
"castle"—a square, three-storied building (Rilke later
spoke of the tower's "embracing quadrate" [2:306])—
which Rilke and Merline visited on 1 July, had no electricity, no running water, and primitive sanitary arrange-

ments; but Rilke was drawn to the tower with a well-nigh mystical fervor.

The negotiations turned out to be complicated because the owner initially demanded an exorbitant price and was reluctant to rent for less than six months; Rilke, with his usual hesitancy about long-term commitments, was unwilling to take it for more than three months and, in his ambivalence, was still toying with invitations from other benefactors. The entire story, which reveals the cunning with which Rilke manipulated his patrons, is spelled out in exhausting detail in the letters that he penned two or three times weekly in a weird creole of French and German to Nanny Wunderly-Volkart, the sisterlike friend who was married to a prosperous manufacturer and whose cousin was the wealthy importer Werner Reinhart. On 4 July, Rilke wrote a long letter describing the discovery of Muzot, the proper local pronunciation of the name ("Muzotte"), the history of the castle, and the difficulties involved with the rental. Four days later he wrote again, saying that it would be sad if Muzot fell through, and inquiring with seeming casualness in the following sentence (with a shift from German to French): Do you have any news of Werner? The very next day he mailed another fretful letter, enclosing a picture postcard of Muzot and assuring Nanny in a frantic shift between languages that he sought nothing but her advice since he was in such a state of indecision: "*Votre conseil*, chère, est la seule chose à laquelle j'aspire: ich bin heute in jenem Zustande der Unentschlossenheit."[24] On 15 July, writing again of his "incertitude atroce" and of the great temptation ("Versuchung") of Muzot, he states that he could probably find nothing to match the tower. Then he asks if Werner has expressed his opinion (as though the family had nothing to think about but Rilke's irresolution). For the first time, he muses that it would be nice if Werner would rent the tower but that he does not "have the heart" to propose it to him. Two pages later, he ponders that perhaps Werner will himself come up with the idea of taking on the negotiations for Muzot.

To no one's surprise (certainly not Rilke's!) Nanny sent him an express letter just two days later announcing Werner's "lovely decision" to rent the tower for a year and place it at Rilke's disposal, for as long or short a period as he wished. (It turned out that Reinhart was already familiar with the tower from a painting he owned.) Of course, Rilke did not accept gracefully and with alacrity: first he needed to equivocate. The next day, he wrote, he lay "as though ill" as his doubts grew almost into despair. But on 20 July he wrote Nanny that he had decided to accept the offer, and included a detailed description of the tower with its beamed ceilings from the seventeenth century and a small chapel that featured a swastika instead of a cross. Now that the negotiations were completed, the next letter (25 July) initiated the second stage of his hints and requests, which continued through the coming weeks: he needs candles, lamps, fabrics, books, and various other items for his new residence—even eau de cologne to scent his bedroom and eau de quinine for his hair!

Under Merline's supervision the tower was cleaned, painted, and equipped—and the rat holes plugged!—in preparation for the poet's arrival, as Rilke reported to Princess Marie on the same 25 July.[25] (Rilke compartmentalized his correspondences: Nanny heard about his physical needs, the princess about his more spiritual ones.) "Tomorrow I shall move out there and make a

Fig. 19. Rainer Maria Rilke on the balcony
at Muzot. Courtesy of Insel Verlag, Frankfurt
am Main.

little attempt at living ("Wohnversuch") in these rather
severe castle conditions, which wrap themselves around
one like a suit of armor! But I had to try it, didn't I,
the way everything happened?" Following a description
of the tower and the various arrangements for his com-
fort the tentative note creeps back into the letter. The
tower and its furnishings, he says, exert a kind of promise
and attraction ("Versprechung und Anziehung") on him:
"if I say attraction, that is not quite precise: because actually all of Muzot, in which something somehow holds
me fast, at the same time also arouses a kind of worry
and oppressiveness ("Sorge und Bedrückung") in my

spirit. . . ." He continues with an account of the history of the château, concluding: "So here, princess, you see me succumbing to ("verfallen") this Muzot, at least for the present: I must make the trial. If only you could see it!"

This sense of mystical obsession, which Rilke called "muzotisme" and "almost a kind of malady,"[26] is expressed repeatedly in the letters from this period. At the end of four weeks he wrote that moving into the tower was like putting on an old suit of armor. During the trial period in July "it was more as though this severe Tour de Muzot were testing me than I it—and I had days of almost being ill and many others at least of apathy, when I couldn't pull myself together, in the battle with the heat and the most immediate inconveniences or at least, let us say, demands of my knightly abode."[27]

But pull himself together he did: by fall he had decided—quite contrary to his original intentions and his usual practice—to remain in Muzot for the winter. Reinhart provided five hundred francs for the necessary winterizing of the tower; a housekeeper (found by Nanny Wunderly-Volkart) was engaged and trained by the solicitous Merline, who in early November departed to spend the winter in Berlin with her sons. (And now that she had helped him find, obtain, and furnish Muzot, she began gradually to disappear from the picture.) Rilke was not entirely deserted by his female friends: in November Nanny arrived in Muzot for a week's visit to assure herself that her poet was faring well. But, in general, he spent the next months in solitude: reading, writing occasional poems, translating Michelangelo's sonnets, carrying on his vast correspondence, and taking long walks in the landscape that he came increasingly to love. But, as he wrote at New Year's to Lou Andreas-Salomé, he still needed time and tranquillity—the "protection"

("Schutz") of his knightly tower—to regain his composure after the many fluctuations and uncertainties of his existence. "An unbelievable difficulty of concentration has remained as a holdover from the interruptedness of the war years; for that reason I cannot survive without the assistance of this literal aloneness."[28]

Then suddenly, following months of indecision, worry, and self-centered indolence, Rilke experienced a three-week surge of creative energy virtually unparalleled in the history of literature. From 2 to 5 February 1922 he wrote the first twenty-five of his *Sonnets to Orpheus* (with one more added on 9 February). After the many letters filled with complaints, vacillations, and requests, Rilke was able to inform Nanny on 8 February that "Something very lovely was given to me, from the 2nd to the 5th of February, for the world: a cycle of *twenty-five* sonnets." Then from 7 to 14 February, working at the second of his two standing desks, he completed the *Duino Elegies*, as he announced in ecstatic letters and telegrams accompanied by copies of various elegies and sonnets. To Anton Kippenberg, on 9 February, he reported that he had gone outside in the cold moonlight and caressed the tower "like a large animal" because it was these old walls that had given him this new inspiration.[29] (He used essentially the same words, this time in French, in a letter that same evening to Merline: "Je suis sorti pour caresser ce vieux Muzot, tout à l'heure au clair de lune."[30] To Nanny on 10 February: "Victory, Victory! *Nine* elegies!" To Princess Marie on 11 February: "finally, the blessed, how blessed day, when I can announce to you the conclusion, as far as I see, of the elegies: *Ten!*"[31] And that same evening to Lou Andreas-Salomé: "At this very moment, this Saturday, the eleventh of February, at 6 o'clock, I put down my pen after the last completed *Elegy*, the tenth."[32] Finally, to his own astonishment, from 15 to 23 February he composed the second part (twenty-four poems) of the *Sonnets to Orpheus*, of which he began circulating copies to his friends. *Mensis mirabilis!*

◨ 7 ◧

Rilke had written the first two of the elegies at Duino exactly ten years earlier (in January and early February 1912); the third, begun at Duino, was finished a year later in Paris; and the fourth was composed in Munich in 1915. All the others, apart from a few verses written in 1912 and 1913, burst forth during the glorious week at Muzot. It is in the elegies written in Muzot that the tower finds its fulfillment as an image in Rilke's oeuvre—an image now freighted with the entire wealth of associations, both cultural and personal, that had accrued to the tower through Rilke's earlier experiences and months of actual residence. As a result, the relevant passages in the poems can be understood in their full intensity only against the background we have sketched to this point.

The elegies constitute a long meditative poem based rhythmically on the elegiac distich as an acknowledgment of their indebtedness to the tradition of the classical German elegy extending back to Goethe and Hölderlin.[33] The elegiac mood permeating the whole cycle reflects Rilke's despair at the loss of unity and security produced in Europe by the social and political upheaval immediately preceding and following World War I. The meditative core is embraced by a personal framework consisting of the First Elegy and the Tenth: the First announces the quandary of the poetic persona and states the principal themes to be treated more fully in the reflective core. It is especially the tension between consciousness and innocence that concerns the poet: humankind has been alienated by partial consciousness from the unity of innocence (exemplified by children, the simple forms of animal life, and the puppet) yet has not attained the unity of full consciousness (exemplified by the angel). In the course of his meditations the reflective self of the elegies is led from an initial state of despair to a level of higher awareness, a moment of anagnorisis, at which he is enabled to see life as a new unity.

The turning point comes in the Fifth Elegy, where Rilke apotheosizes the acrobats (inspired by Picasso's painting *Les Saltimbanques*) whose growing skill transports them from poignant inadequacy to empty virtuosity. Turning to the angel, the poet longs for a place, an inexpressible carpet, on which lovers and acrobats could attain "their bold lofty figures of heart-leaps, their towers of desire":

> Engel!: Es wäre ein Platz, den wir nicht wissen,
>   und dorten,
> auf unsäglichem Teppich, zeigten die Liebenden,
>   die's hier
> bis zum Können nie bringen, ihre kühnen
> hohen Figuren des Herzschwungs,
> ihre Türme aus Lust. . . .   (1:705)

(Angel! there might be a place that we know nothing about, and there, / on an ineffable carpet, the lovers, who here / never quite attain the ability, display the bold / lofty patterns of their soaring hearts, / their towers of desire.)

In the Seventh Elegy the image of eroticism gives way as the poet attains the crucial insight of the cycle: that it is the responsibility of poets not to compete with the angels in the realm of feelings, where they are supreme, but to praise the excellence of earthly existence—"Hiersein ist herrlich"—by internalizing earthly reality into a mode that the angel can apprehend. And into this "Weltinnenraum" he sets as the first great image a tower—the long-remembered tower from the cathedral at Chartres.

So haben wir dennoch
nicht die Räume versäumt, diese gewährenden,
diese
unseren Räume. (Was müssen sie fürchterlich
groß sein,
da sie Jahrtausende nicht unseres Fühlns überfülln.)
Aber ein Turm war groß, nicht wahr? O Engel,
er war es,—
groß, auch noch neben dir? Chartres war groß—,
und Musik
reichte noch weiter hinan und überstieg uns.

(1:712)

(So we haven't after all / missed out on the spaces, these indulgent spaces, these / spaces *of ours*. [How frightfully large they must be, / since centuries of our feeling have not filled them up.] / But one tower was great, wasn't it? O Angel, it was,—/great, even compared to you. Chartres was great—, and music / went even higher and climbed beyond us.)

This is the poet's task, he concludes in the Ninth Elegy: to praise what is here, those things that exist on earth just one time and that therefore require our utterance for their preservation. Again he lists examples of objects that need us to rescue them through the internalization of language, adding punningly in conclusion as the highest objects: pillar and tower.

> Sind wir vielleicht *hier*, um zu sagen: Haus,
> Brücke, Brunnen, Tor, Krug, Obstbaum,
>   Fenster,—
> höchstens: Säule, Turm. . . . aber zu *sagen*, verstehs,
> oh zu sagen *so*, wie selber die Dinge niemals
> innig meinten zu sein.   (1:718)

> (Are we perhaps *here* just to say: house, / bridge,
> well, gate, jug, fruit-tree, window,— / at most
> pillar, tower . . . but to *say* them, you see, / oh, to
> say them *so* fervently as the things themselves /
> never thought themselves capable of being.)

Not surprisingly, the tower figures centrally in Rilke's own exegesis of the elegies. As he was to explain to his Polish translator a year before his death:

> The angel of the *Elegies* is that creature in whom the transformation of the visible into the invisible that we seek to accomplish has already been completed. For the angel of the elegies all past towers and palaces are existent *because* they have long been invisible, and the towers and bridges of our existence that still have being are *already* invisible although still (for us) physically present.[34]

◫ 8 ◫

As Rilke completed the elegies in his tower at Muzot, then, the tower forced itself upon his consciousness as a central image of human desire, of human achievement, and of those earthly things that the poet has the responsibility of internalizing and eternalizing in language in order to justify his existence vis-à-vis the angel. At this point poetry and the poet's life have become so wholly interwoven that the tower at Muzot becomes the instantiation of all the towers present in Rilke's earlier poetry— as landmark, as *Ding*, as consciousness, as expression of desire. Entering his tower, Rilke enters and reenacts all the associations that have become attached to towers in his poetic imagination since his childhood in Prague. Rilke was fully aware of the role that Muzot played in his poetic life. (In May 1922 Reinhart bought the tower outright and gave it to the poet for his lifetime use.) In 1924 he explained to a correspondent that he had traveled very little in the postwar years. "Since Muzot was found, I have clung stubbornly to a settled way of life because I immediately understood that this place was bestowed upon me in order that I might accomplish in precise summary all that had been interrupted and endangered in my own work for years."[35] A year before his death he told another correspondent that he had become more and more closely bound to his tower and to the grandiose landscape of the Valais, and that he regarded his presence there as "the most wondrous providence" ("die wunderbarste Fügung").[36] The circumstances of the war years, he continues, and his own inner numbness had prevented him from continuing the elegies begun in 1912. "Nowhere but here, in the Valais, . . . could such a supply of unsuspected assistance be gathered: for here there took place—and everything was helpful—in the severe loneliness of the winter of 1921– 1922, the scarcely hoped-for connection to the fractured work of 1914, and it was so pure and so passionate, and at the same time of such a healing mildness, that the entirety of the elegies arose from a few weeks of indescribable devotion." Even when he was forced by his illness to retreat to the sanatorium at Val-Mont, he felt reassured by the fact that "I am only three hours from my old tower, where I belonged, and yet still don't dare to return out of the fear that I am not equal to its strict rules of solitude."[37] In the troubled years of the early 1920s[38]— as the French occupied the Rhineland, as inflation undermined Rilke's sources of support, as political turmoil split Germany and caused the assassination of Walter Rathenau, as controversy surrounded his latest work, as his political views became so conservative that he cast admiring eyes on Mussolini's accomplishments in Italy, as he was tormented increasingly by the leukemia that finally caused his death—the tower at Muzot represented for Rilke more and more a point of stability in the midst of chaos. As he confided to yet another of his admiring princesses: "Midnight at Muzot sometimes really brings a sense of superiority of the things and walls occupied with their past."[39]

Other towers occur in Rilke's late poems from Muzot. In a witty poem written at Christmastime 1921, "For Werner Reinhart" (to whom he referred jocularly as his "liege lord" ["Lehensmann"]),[40] the poet invokes the theme of Noah and the ark to express his appreciation to his benefactor and to make it seem that his own skillful manipulation of his benefactors had been the work of God. After his expulsion from the ark at Berg, it begins, he invoked the Lord for another vessel. And the Lord, listening to his prayer, drove the mice out of a tower that had nurtured them, and showed him the "curable housing" that had been painted years earlier for Reinhart by an artist. Then the Lord, who leaves nothing to

chance, called Reinhart and gave them a hundred signs
that Muzot was destined for them both, the poet and
his benefactor.

Und er erhörte mich und trieb die Mäuse
aus einem Turm, der ihnen Nahrung war,
und zeigte mir das heilbare Gehäuse,
das eines Malers Hand vor manchem Jahr
für *Sie* gemalt. Dann rief er Sie desgleichen,
der nirgends einen Zufall kennt, der Gott,
und überhäufte uns mit hundert Zeichen
das endlich doch gebotene Muzot.   (2:248)

Towers also play a role in several of the other poems
that Rilke wrote during the Muzot years, as he turned
increasingly to French—in his reading, in his letters, and
in his own writing. In one of the "Quatrains Valaisans,"
for instance, a church tower boasts that, superior to any
mere "tour profane" (such as Muzot), it ripens its sweet
carillon song for the people of the Valais (2:561). Another
recounts the proud forlornness of the towers of the Valais
as they recall the days of their loftier existence:

Fier abandon de ces tours
qui pourtant se souviennent
—depuis quand jusqu'à toujours—
de leur vie aérienne."   (2:567)

But none expresses Rilke's lifelong obsession with towers,
which ripened from simple background by way of an
image for the emergence of consciousness to the expression of the human condition in all its desire, anxiety, and
achievement, as completely and powerfully as the towers
of the *Duino Elegies.* Driven by a mystical urge to actual-
ize the image that had filled his poems for a quarter-

century, Rilke moved into the tower of Muzot. Once within his tower, he was inspired in turn by its accumulated associations to create the great poems in which finally the image found its most appropriate, compressed, and vivid place.

Carl Gustav Jung: The Tower of the Psyche

Fig. 20. The first tower at Bollingen, built in 1923. Aniela Jaffé, ed.,
C. G. Jung: Word and Image. Copyright 1979 by Princeton University
Press. Reprinted by permission of Princeton University Press.

If Yeats, Jeffers, and Rilke are the poets of the tower, then Carl Gustav Jung (1875–1961) is surely its philosopher— or more accurately, perhaps, its psychographer. It is symptomatic of the importance he attached to towers in his own life and thought that Jung devoted an entire chapter of his memoirs[1] to the tower at Bollingen, a "confession of faith in stone" (223), which he built over a period of some thirty years, and the stages of whose construction reflect major crises in his life. Although the tower does not hold a privileged position among the images and archetypes of his analytical psychology, it emerges in his personal life as the predominant site and symbol of his thought.

In Jung's case, as in Jeffers's, the tower cannot be separated from the well-nigh mystical feeling he had for stones. Readers of his scholarly works know what a central position stones occupy in his thought: the philosopher's stone or *lapis philosophorum* as the goal of the alchemist's pursuits (in *Psychology and Alchemy* and *Alchemical Studies*); the stone as an image of Christ (in *Alchemical Studies* and *Aion*); the stone as a symbol of the unified self (in *Aion* and *The Archetypes and the Collective Unconscious*). The indexes to his Collected Works constitute a veritable quarry of references.[2]

This lapidary mysticism belongs among Jung's most primal experiences. In the first chapter of his memoirs he describes a pastime that he invented as a boy of seven or eight years. Beyond the garden wall of his father's parsonage in Klein-Hüningen near Basel lay a slope in which a large stone was embedded.

> Often, when I was alone, I sat down on this stone, and then began an imaginary game that went something like this: "I am sitting on top of this stone and it is underneath." But the stone also could say "I" and think: "I am lying here on this slope and he is sitting on top of me." The question then arose: "Am I the one who is sitting on the stone, or am I the stone on which *he* is sitting?" (20)

Although the answer always remained unclear, even as a child Jung had "no doubt whatsoever that this stone stood in some secret relationship to me." Thirty years later, when he returned to his boyhood home as a married man with children of his own and a place in the world, the sight of that stone with its secret significance still had the power to make his life in Zurich seem alien, remote, and temporally bound.

Among the major icons of Jung's childhood, which he hid in the attic under the roof beams, were a tiny carved manikin of wood and "a smooth, oblong blackish stone from the Rhine" (21), which stood in the same relationship to each other as did Jung and his stone on the slope outside: in each case the stone provided "a supply of life-force" (23). The symbolic relationship to stones, as we shall see, remained a consistent theme in Jung's psychic life. "At any time in my later life when I got stuck, I painted a picture or hewed stone" (175; *ETG*, 178). In his memoirs, accordingly, Jung tells us that words and paper gradually came to seem inadequate for the expression of his thoughts. "I had to achieve a kind of representation in stone of my innermost thoughts and of the knowledge I had acquired. Or, to put it another way, I had to make a confession of faith in stone. That was the beginning of the 'Tower,' the house which I built for myself at Bollingen" (223).

Jung bought his land on the upper Lake Zurich in 1922, just at the time when, unbeknownst to him, Rilke was experiencing epiphanies in his own tower just to the south across the Alps. For several summers (1918–1923) Jung had vacationed with his family on a small island at the upper end of Lake Zurich, where he and his children lived in tents and played at being pirates in the various boats at their disposal.[3] Attracted by the charm of the landscape, he bought the property at Bollingen with the intention originally of building some sort of primitive one-story dwelling like an African hut. But soon his plans became more ambitious.

Like stones, the image of towers had also played a prominent role in Jung's boyhood amusements and dreams. His first memory of games, he recalls in his memoirs, dated from his seventh or eighth year (around the time of his mystical experience with the stone on the slope outside). "I was passionately fond of playing with bricks, and built towers which I then rapturously destroyed by an 'earthquake'" (18). Later, during his school years, Jung cultivated a recurrent vision during his walks from Klein-Hüningen into Basel: of a hill rising out of a lake and, at its top, a castle with a tall keep or watchtower.

The nerve center and *raison d'être* of this whole arrangement was the secret of the keep, which I alone knew. . . . inside the tower, extending from the battlements to the vaulted cellar, was a copper column or heavy wire cable, which ramified at the top into the finest branches, like the crown of a tree or—better still—like a taproot with all its tiny rootlets turned upside down and reaching into the air. From the air they drew a certain unimaginable Something which was conducted down the copper column into the cellar. Here I had an equally unimaginable apparatus, a kind of laboratory in which I made gold out of the mysterious substance which the copper roots drew from the air. (81; *ETG*, 86–87)

This vision anticipates the serious scholarly interest in alchemy that Jung developed many years later. But above all the tower itself represented "an arcanum, of whose nature I neither had nor wished to form any conception."

◨ 2 ◨

Jung's almost instinctive decision to build a tower of stone on his plot of lakeside land was thus clearly an outgrowth of dreams and visions that had gripped him since childhood. An additional factor needs to be taken into account, however, if we are to appreciate the full significance of the tower at Bollingen. On the trip to the United States that Jung and Freud undertook in 1909, the two men were in the habit of regularly analyzing each other's dreams. Jung reports that Freud had great difficulty interpreting certain dreams that Jung was having at that time—"dreams with collective contents, containing a great deal of symbolic material" (158). One dream in particular held special significance for Jung because it suggested to him the new concept of the "collective unconscious" that informed his book *Psychology of the Unconscious* (1912; later revised as *Symbols of Transformation*) and precipitated the falling-out with Freud. In his memoirs (158–61) Jung describes in detail the dream, which revolved around a house: a two-story building with stairs leading down to a vaulted cellar; in the stone floor of the cellar a movable slab exposing stone steps descending into the dark depths; in the cave at the bottom, bones and broken pottery and two human skulls. Freud, it seems, was interested chiefly in the two skulls and tried to focus the analysis exclusively on them. But Jung had a different view. "It was plain to me that the house represented a kind of image of the psyche"—from the consciousness represented by the upstairs salon, by way of the first level of the unconscious (the medieval decor of the ground floor) and an earlier level implicit in the Roman foundations of the cellar, down to the prehistoric cave, where he found the remains of a primitive culture: "the world of the primitive man within myself—a world which can scarcely be reached or illuminated by consciousness." The dream-house, in sum, symbolized the stages of consciousness not only of mankind as a whole but of Jung as an individual—a collective interpretation utterly alien to Freud, who sought to reduce the entire panorama to an image more consistent with his own psychoanalytical theories: that is, a death wish suggested by the two skulls.

The building as an image for the psyche became predominant in Jung's thought. In the years before he discovered alchemy, for instance, Jung had a recurrent dream that dealt with a similar theme. Attached to his house he saw another unfamiliar wing or annex that in the course of several dreams he was unable to reach. Finally his dream-self entered the foreign wing and discovered a library of large folio volumes from the sixteenth and seventeenth centuries, illustrated with curious symbols that he did not recognize. (They turned out later to be alchemical symbols.) "The unknown wing of the house was a part of my personality," Jung later understood, "an aspect of myself; it represented something that belonged to me but of which I was not yet conscious" (202). In a lecture entitled "Mind and Earth" ("Seele und Erde," 1927) Jung elaborates this analogy more fully:

> [We must] describe and explain a building whose upper storey was erected in the nineteenth century, the ground floor dates back to the sixteenth century, and a careful examination of the masonry reveals that it was reconstructed from a tower built in the eleventh century. In the cellar we come upon Roman foundations, and under the cellar a choked-up cave with neolithic tools in the upper layer and remnants of fauna from the same period in the lower layers. That would be the picture of our psychic structure: We live on the upper storey and are only dimly aware that the lower is slightly old-fashioned. As to what lies beneath the earth's surface, of that we remain totally unconscious.[4]

Now that we understand the importance for Jung of stone as an image of the life force, of the tower as the preserve of the arcanum, and of architecture as a reflection of the self, we are prepared to appreciate the full significance of the stone tower that Jung built at Bollingen. For this tower of the psyche was undertaken at a critical point in Jung's intellectual and emotional development. Following the break with Freud in 1913, Jung resigned as president of the International Psychoanalytical Association, gave up his lectureship at the University of Zurich, and entered a period of intense introversion—the period that in his memoirs he calls his "confrontation with the unconscious" ("Auseinandersetzung mit dem Unbewußten"). He later regarded these years as the most important of his life: years that provided, he said, the *prima materia* (199; *ETG*, 203: "Urstoff") for a lifetime's work. The period was punctuated by a year of enormous intellectual fertility: in 1916 he transcribed his inner experiences in the richly illustrated folio of his so-called Red Book[5] and summed them up in his privately published *Septem Sermones ad Mortuos*; he drew the first of the mandalas (symbols of human wholeness) that were to occupy him for many years; he began the serious study of Gnosticism; and he first conceived and began to use certain key terms that characterize his analytical psychology: animus/ anima, persona, individuation, and collective unconscious. This outburst of creative energies was succeeded by a fallow period from which he finally emerged in 1921 with the publication of *Psychological Types*. The tower at Bollingen, begun soon thereafter, can thus be regarded as the realization in stone of Jung's own sense of self (a term first used in *Psychological Types*) when he came out of what he called the "darkness" (195, 199) of those years of intense introspection.

◻ 3 ◻

In 1923 Jung undertook the construction of his first round tower. In the Bollingen quarry with the assistance of two Italian masons he learned, like Jeffers, how to split stones and soon became skillful in the art of stone-

Fig. 21. The tower-complex at Bollingen in 1956. Aniela Jaffé, ed., *C. G. Jung: Word and Image*. Copyright 1979 by Princeton University Press. Reprinted by permission of Princeton University Press.

masonry.[6] From the very start he felt an intense sense of "repose and renewal" (224), of "security" ("Geborgensein"; *ETG*, 227), in the tower, which was completed in the winter of 1923–24. Begun as it was just two months after his mother's death, "It represented for me the maternal hearth" (224). As he wrote two years later, "I just spent about 3 weeks in the tower, where I finished the 3rd edition of a little book of mine, much inspired by the peculiar atmosphere of the place."[7] In the following decades Jung often spent as much as half of each year in his private sanctuary rather than in the family home in Küsnacht near Zurich.

That first building became the cornerstone for the complex of structures and towers that Jung erected, with consciously numerological and geometrical symbolism, in the course of more than thirty years. Jung tells us that he became increasingly aware that the first tower "did not yet express everything that needed saying" (224). Accordingly, in 1927 he added a central structure with a tower-like annex. After another interval of four years, again sensing incompleteness, he extended the annex. "I wanted a room in this tower where I could exist for myself alone" (224). To this meditation chamber Jung kept the only key and allowed others to enter only with his permission. "Thus the second tower became for me a place of spiritual concentration" (224).

Four years later, in 1935, he was seized by the desire for an enclosure—but a space open to the sky and nature. So he added to the round tower and the central structure with its towerlike annex a courtyard and a loggia by the lake as a fourth element. "Thus a quaternity had arisen, four different parts of the building, and, moreover, in the course of twelve years" (224–25). As a quaternity, needless to say, the tower-complex constituted an architectural analogy to the mandala, whose basic pattern is the circle divided into four parts. "The quaternity is an archetype of almost universal occurrence," Jung wrote later in *Psychology and Religions*. "The ideal of completeness is the circle or sphere, but its natural minimal division is a quaternity."[8]

After twelve years the numerological-geometrical phase was completed, but Jung's own consciousness had not yet stopped its growth. The first tower, as I have mentioned, was begun two months after the death of his mother. Following his wife's death in 1955 he "suddenly realized that the small central section which crouched so low, so hidden, was myself! I could no longer hide myself behind the 'maternal' and the 'spiritual' towers. So, in that same year, I added an upper story to this section, which represents myself, or my ego-personality. . . . an extension of consciousness achieved in old age" (225). Although Jung built his house section by section in response to the exigencies of the moment, he regarded the tower from the beginning as "a place of maturation—a maternal womb or a maternal figure in which I could be myself as I am, was, and will be. It gave me a feeling as if I were being reborn in stone. It appeared to me like a concretization of earlier premonitions and a representation of the individuation process. A memorial *aere perennius*" (225; *ETG,* 229). Only later did he see in it "a symbol of psychic wholeness" (225). "There is nothing in the Tower that has not grown into its own form over the decades, nothing with which I am not linked" (226).

At Bollingen, Jung writes, "I am in the midst of my most essential being, I am most profoundly myself" (225; *ETG,* 229). But the tower is not simply the image of personal ontogeny; it also recapitulates the phylogeny of the race. "At times I feel as if I am spread out over the landscape and inside things, and am myself living in every tree, . . . silence surrounds me almost audibly, and I live 'in modest harmony with nature.' Thoughts rise to the surface which reach back into the centuries, and accordingly anticipate a remote future" (225–26). More even than Yeats, Jeffers, and Rilke, Jung was aware of the ancient symbolism of the tower as a place of religious experience, of introspection, of astrological investigation, of refuge—and he explored all these aspects fully in the various emblems with which, like Jeffers, he decorated the tower and its precincts.

◨ 4 ◨

First among these is the stone monument that he created in 1950 to express the *genius loci* of the complex. Recapitulating his childhood experience, Jung found himself in a mystical relationship to a large square stone which had been sent from the quarry mistakenly instead of the triangular stone that had been specified. When the mason wanted to send it back, Jung intervened, sensing that he was destined to do something special and personal with the stone. Gradually he chiseled words and images onto its faces: first a Latin verse by the alchemist Arnaldus de Villanova; then a large eye with a tiny homunculus in its pupil representing the psychagogue; facing the lake a Latin inscription quoted from alchemistic texts; and finally a Latin *fecit* by Jung in remembrance of his seventy-fifth birthday in 1950 (like the *fecit* that Jeffers set in Hawk Tower). "The stone stands outside the Tower, and is like an explanation of it. It is a manifestation of the occupant, but one which remains incomprehensible to others" (228). As he put it later, "The stone belongs to its secluded place between lake and hill, where it expresses the *beata solitudo* and the *genius loci*, the spell of the chosen and walled-in spot."[9]

Five years later, in the winter of 1955–56, Jung chiseled the names of his paternal ancestors on three stone tablets and placed them in the courtyard of the tower (232). At the same time he painted the ceiling with motifs from his own and his wife's coats of arms: a cross and a bunch of grapes symbolizing the spirits of heaven and earth united by a gold star, the *aurum philosophorum*. These Masonic and Rosicrucian images, placed in the armorial field by

Jung's grandfather, suggest "the historical nexus of my thinking and my life" (232). Jung concluded, namely, that his seventeenth-century ancestor Dr. Carl Jung of Mainz, a physician, would have been familiar with the writings of two well-known contemporary alchemists who lived in nearby Frankfurt, and that therefore Jung's own arcane researches into alchemy stemmed unconsciously from a long-standing family tradition. In any case, as he was working on the stone tablets, he became aware of the links between himself and his ancestors. "I feel very strongly that I am under the influence of things or questions which were left incomplete and unanswered by my parents and grandparents and more distant ancestors" (233). In this connection Jung speaks of an "impersonal karma" within a family that is passed on from parents to children. He goes on to conjecture that his own researches were meant to answer questions "which fate had posed to my forefathers and which had not yet been answered"—a collective problem, in sum, that had become a personal concern. The tower thus functions in Jung's mind, as in the Minoan *nuraghi* (which he does not mention), as a concrete link back to the dead. He acknowledged as much in his memoirs, pointing out that the tower was begun following the death of his mother and completed after the death of his wife. "These two dates are meaningful because the Tower, as we shall see, is connected with the dead" (225).

The spirit of the tower led Jung to a further speculation. There had long been a (completely unfounded) family rumor that Jung's grandfather was an illegitimate son of Goethe's. Ever since his boyhood, when his mother suggested that he read *Faust*, Jung had been fascinated by the polarity in Goethe's masterpiece between

Faust and Mephistopheles, between good and evil—and in particular by what struck Jung as the sinful behavior of Faust toward Philemon and Baucis, the aged couple that he permits to be killed at the end of Goethe's poetic drama so that he can obtain their little plot of land. It suddenly became clear to Jung that he had "taken over *Faust as my heritage*": that he was to serve as the advocate and avenger of Philemon and Baucis; that the figure of Philemon had become "a personal matter between me and *proavus* Goethe"; indeed, that it was his responsibility to give an answer to the terrible Faustian problem that devastated Europe during the Second World War.[10] "I consciously linked my work to what Faust had passed over: respect for the eternal rights of man, recognition of 'the ancient,' and the continuity of culture and intellectual history" (235). During these years of introspection the figure of Philemon emerged more prominently in Jung's fantasies as the embodiment of the wise old man who serves as his spiritual guide: he tells us that he held conversations with Philemon, who said things that he had not consciously thought (183). Representing superior insight, Philemon became Jung's psychagogue and communicated to him many illuminating ideas. It seems inevitable, therefore, that Jung should carve above the entrance to the first tower at Bollingen the inscription *Philemonis Sacrum. Fausti Poenitentia* (Philemon's Sanctuary. Faust's Penitence).[11] When that inscription was walled up in the course of the expansion, he had the words carved over the entrance to the second tower to suggest yet another dimension of meaning.

The tower precincts contain other relief carvings of various archetypal images: a female bear pushing a round stone (symbolizing the power and energy of Artemis); a primitive woman milking a mare ("obviously my anima in the guise of a millennia-old ancestress"); and an inscription anticipating the coming of Pegasus or the Age of Aquarius.[12] Finally, the wall displays the malicious smile of the Trickster, the psyche at its level of an absolutely undifferentiated human consciousness, as Jung described it in his essay "On the Psychology of the Trickster Figure" (1954),[13] and known universally in folklore and fairy tales. Jung, with his profound belief in archetypes, sought to unmask and disarm the Trickster by carving him out in stone. "I thought that I had laid him, but I was obviously wrong again."[14]

In the course of the years, finally, Jung decorated the rooms within the tower with murals and thus "expressed all those things which have carried me out of time into seclusion, out of the present into timelessness" (224)—in short, archetypes of the sort whose models first appeared in his "Red Book." According to the report of one visitor, "One could hardly sleep in one's bed there at night, so alive and urgent was his presence in the murals around the room."[15]

▣ 5 ▣

Clearly the tower at Bollingen is a space with many dimensions and aspects, including and summarizing almost all the associations that we have previously seen—personal, ancestral, collective. A place for introspection and retreat, it exemplifies the personal psyche and the various stages of its consciousness. It is the retreat to which, in the course of forty years, Jung withdrew for weeks and

Fig. 22. Carl Gustav Jung at Bollingen in 1958. Aniela Jaffé, ed. *C. G. Jung: Word and Image.* Copyright 1979 by Princeton University Press. Reprinted by permission of Princeton University Press.

months at a time to engage the mysteries of his own psyche. In the profound solitude of Bollingen with its murals exemplifying his soul, Jung chopped the wood, tended the fire, pumped the water, cooked the food, and read by the old lamps that he lit himself, gradually succumbing to the ancestral tablets and icons that linked him to the past—to his "alchemistic" forefathers as well as to his *proavus* Goethe. And beyond the individual and the family, the wall reliefs embody the archetypes of anima, trickster, and others that constitute the collective memory of humankind as a whole.

Jung's concluding paragraph to his chapter on the tower in his memoirs summarizes movingly the meaning of the tower in his life and thought.

> In the Tower at Bollingen it is as if one lived in many centuries simultaneously. The place will outlive me, and in its location and style it points backward to things of long ago. There is very little about it to suggest the present. . . . There is nothing to disturb the dead, neither electric light nor telephone. Moreover, my ancestors' souls are sustained by the spiritual atmosphere of the house, since I answer for them the questions that their lives once left behind. I carve out rough answers as best I can. I have even drawn them on the walls. It is as if a silent, greater family, stretching down the centuries, were peopling the house. There I live in my second personality and see life in the round, as something forever coming into being and passing on. (237; *ETG*, 241)

CHAPTER SIX

The Broken Towers

Fig. 23. Kaiser Wilhelm Memorial Church, Berlin.
Courtesy of Yetta Ziolkowski.

◙ 1 ◙

Our survey of the modern landscape of literary towers has brought to light a number of fascinating parallels among individual figures. Most obvious, perhaps, is the lapidary mysticism of Jeffers and Jung—the all but religious sense of identification that enabled Jung to project himself vicariously into the consciousness of the stone upon which he was sitting and that inspired Jeffers to give voice to the ancient stones of Mycenae, for whom human beings are the active creatures "that have two ends let downward." Both men appeared to be most content when they were working with stone, building over decades their tower complexes with no electricity to upset the circadian cycles of life and with no telephones that would enable the outside world to intrude upon their meditations. Both decorated the rooms and walls of their stone habitations with carvings and objects that transformed their dwellings into externalized expressions of their innermost being. And for both men the tower held a mystical association with the women in their lives.

But other parallels are conspicuous as well. Yeats and Jeffers both identified with their towers, which Yeats specifically called his symbol, and portray themselves, in "The Tower" and in "Margrave," leaning on the balustrades and meditating upon past and future. (Rilke, objectifying the tower as distinct from himself, is the outsider here: when he completed his Elegies, he went outside and stroked his tower as though it were a large animal.) Yeats, who like Rilke came to his own tower as the fulfillment of years-long wishes, shares with Rilke the conception of the climb up the tower as the gyrelike ascent of consciousness. And the spiritual detachment of the angel that Rilke finally came to acknowledge in Muzot resembles on the one hand the attitude of "inhumanism" that Jeffers recommended and on the other the wisdom of Jung's Philemon.

Beyond these individual parallels, certain common factors have emerged that characterize the four writers as a group. All of the same generation (born between 1865 and 1887), they became disenchanted with the degeneration of a world that all, as young men, had eagerly embraced. Yeats's lament for an age when "The best lack all conviction, while the worst / Are full of passionate intensity" ("The Second Coming") is simply the most famous expression of the moral criticism that informs many of his poems. In "Teheran" (in *The Double Axe*) Jeffers invites us to "Observe also / How rapidly civilization coarsens and decays; its better qualities, foresight, humaneness, disinterested / Respect for truth, die first; its worst will be last" (3:125). Rilke (in the Tenth Elegy) portrays modern society as a City of Suffering ("Leid-Stadt") marked by gilded noise and bursting monuments ("der vergoldete Lärm, das platzende Denkmal"). And Jung believed that "Our Western intellectualistic and rationalistic attitude has gradually become a sickness causing disturbances of the psychic equilibrium to an extent that can hardly be estimated at present."[1] This disenchantment became so powerful that in all four cases it led, after World War I, to a position of political conservatism that has been attacked by their critics as fascist:[2] Rilke's late admiration of

Mussolini, the marching songs that Yeats wrote for the Blueshirt Party, the bitter and often intemperate railing of Jeffers's *The Double Axe*, and Jung's justifications of his dealings with Nazi Germany.[3]

What is unique about these four, however, is not their analysis of postwar society and culture, which was shared by many modernists; it is their response to it. All four built or retreated shortly after World War I into towers that were conspicuously spiritual refuges: the mystical values associated with the image were in each case much more consequential than the architectural dimensions of the rather squat structures at Ballylee, Carmel, Muzot, and Bollingen. In each case the retreat was triggered by the horror of World War I and its sequel. For each, in his characteristic way, the tower became an icon of consciousness or psyche or desire. And all four chose to emphasize and thematize the centrality of the tower in their thought by dedicating specific works to their stone habitations: Yeats's *The Tower* and *The Winding Stair*; Jeffers's various poems on building with stone and the framework of "Margrave" and other works; Rilke's "Der Turm" along with his Elegies; and Jung's chapter on "The Tower" in his memoirs.

There is no evidence, however, of any influence among the four writers in the common turriphilia dominating their lives and works. Jeffers, the youngest, is the only one who was acquainted with the works and reputations of the other three: Yeats became one of his favorite poets; Una read Rilke intensively during the 1930s[4] and no doubt communicated her knowledge, if not her enthusiasm, to her husband; around the time of World War I Jeffers familiarized himself with the work of Jung (and

Freud).[5] But he became interested in Yeats only after he had built his own tower—perhaps, indeed, as a result of that enterprise—and he was unaware of Jung's simultaneous tower building at Bollingen. None of the European writers, however, was aware of Jeffers. Rilke knew neither Jung nor Yeats. Late in his life Jung became interested in Rilke[6] but seems not to have known that the poet had also lived in a tower; although he owned a copy of Yeats's *A Vision,* Jung claimed never to have read a line by his Irish contemporary.[7] There is no firm evidence that Yeats, despite obvious correspondences in their ideas (and the presence of Jung's *Analytical Psychology* in his library), had actually read Jung;[8] and while his late letters (fall 1938) refer to a collection of essays on Rilke, he nowhere alludes to a firsthand acquaintance with Rilke's poetry. So we must attribute their postwar turn to towers to factors in their individual biographies and to their undisputed familiarity with the Western cultural tradition, in which towers played a distinct role.

◫ 2 ◫

Rilke left the Château de Muzot in 1926 only to die, and Yeats relinquished Thoor Ballylee three years later for reasons of health. Jung and Jeffers inhabited the towers they built until their respective deaths in 1961 and 1962. Yet in the very year when Jung bought his plot of land at Bollingen and when Rilke was singing the praise of towers in the *Duino Elegies,* T. S. Eliot in *The Waste Land* (1922) employed the image to proclaim his vision of a disintegrating civilization:

What is the city over the mountains
Cracks and reforms and bursts in the violet air
Falling towers
Jerusalem Athens Alexandria
Vienna London
Unreal[9]

It is hardly an accident that in another defining modernist work, Joyce's *Ulysses* (1922), Stephen Dedalus abandons the Martello tower at Sandycove, which he has been sharing with Buck Mulligan, to depart into his second exile. This tower, which Mulligan regards as a temple of neopaganism, "omphalos," and where Dedalus has isolated himself from family, church, and society, represents precisely the kind of Celtic romanticism, still flourishing in 1904, that he now, following his encounter with reality in the person of Leopold Bloom, chooses to leave behind. Like Maleine and Axël, Dedalus descends from the symbolist tower—not to die, however, but to set out in search of an authentic life and art.

The inherent ambiguity of the image—preserve of spirit and platform of arrogance, shelter of virtue and hideaway of sexuality, epitome of steadfastness no firmer than the foundation on which it is built—had of course been present from the beginnings. But it was suppressed during most of the nineteenth century in favor of the image of the proud tower. In a celebrated passage of his *Pensées*, which provided the title for Erich Kahler's penetrating "inquiry into the transformation of the individual" (*The Tower and the Abyss*, 1957), Pascal characterized human reason as suspended between two extremes or infinities—mind and body, spirit and nature—and unable to comprehend either. "We are consumed by the desire to find a firm position and an ultimate steady base upon which to build a tower that will rise to the infinite; but our whole foundation bursts, and the earth opens to its very abysses."[10]

Sir James Frazer varied that image of ambiguity in the introduction to the second edition of *The Golden Bough*, published at the turn of the century. Frazer acknowledged that the comparative study of the beliefs and institutions of mankind, while providing a powerful instrument for progress and enlightenment, can also shatter precious beliefs.

> It is indeed a melancholy and in some respects thankless task to strike at the foundations of beliefs in which, as in a strong tower, the hopes and aspirations of humanity through long ages have sought a refuge from the storm and stress of life. Yet sooner or later it is inevitable that the battery of the comparative method should breach these venerable walls, mantled over with the ivy and mosses and wild flowers of a thousand tender and sacred associations.[11]

It was not just the forces of comparative religion, as popularized by the Theosophical Society, that were undermining the foundations upon which the proud towers of the nineteenth century had securely rested. In the decade before World War I, Einstein challenged Newtonian conceptions of time and space in thought experiments that were validated soon after the war. The ideas of Freud, Marx, and Nietzsche were transforming humankind's understanding of the self, the social world, and the spiritual world that had once been a source of faith.[12] The nonobjective art of Kandinsky and Klee moved beyond the boundaries of representation still observed by prewar cubism; while the serial compositions of Webern, Alban Berg, and Schönberg discarded the tonalities that still informed the compositions of Mahler, Stravinsky, and Debussy. World War I tore down any remaining social and spiritual barriers that had precluded the total permeation of these modernist forms and ideas and released in addition the forces of ethnic nationalism, communism, and fascism, which washed away the remnants of nineteenth-century empire. Shortly after the war Thomas Mann summed up the feelings of his generation in his lecture "Goethe and Tolstoy" (1922), stating that, since the Russian Revolution, "in the European West, too, the sense has arisen that not only for Russia but for the whole world an epoch is coming to an end: the bürgerlich-humanist-liberal epoch that, born in the Renaissance, came to power with the French Revolution and whose last gasps and throes we are witnessing."[13] As a result, modernists like Eliot and Joyce saw the proud towers of the nineteenth century with different eyes—as falling, as collapsing structures, as artificial retreats to be abandoned.

▣ 3 ▣

In a talk delivered in 1940, a year before her death, Virginia Woolf resorted to the familiar topos to distinguish writers of the postwar years from those who came to maturity before 1914. Characterizing the older generation, she wrote:

> He sits upon a tower raised above the rest of us; a tower built first on his parents' station, then on his

parents' gold. It is a tower of the utmost importance; it decides his angle of vision; it affects his power of communication.

All through the nineteenth century, down to August 1914, that tower was a steady tower.[14]

At the end of the war, however, the tower that had sustained generations of poets no longer stood straight. The younger poets, still the well-educated sons of prosperous parents, also inhabited the towers of privilege.

But what a difference in the tower itself, in what they saw from the tower! When they looked at human life what did they see? Everywhere change; everywhere revolution. In Germany, in Russia, in Italy, in Spain, all the old hedges were being rooted up; all the old towers were being thrown to the ground. Other hedges were being planted; other towers were being raised. There was communism in one country; in another fascism. The whole of civilisation, of society, was changing. . . . even in England towers that were built of gold and stucco were no longer steady towers. They were leaning towers.[15]

A decade earlier, in *To the Lighthouse* (1927), Virginia Woolf showed how completely the tower had been exhausted of its traditional associations. Having become an empty image, it symbolizes the goal of varying aspirations of the Ramsay family. For the serene, beautiful, and practical-minded Mrs. Ramsay, the point of the expedition to the tower is a mundane mission of mercy: to deliver needed goods and magazines to the isolated inhabitants of the lighthouse. For Mr. Ramsay, the rational philosopher, the tower becomes no more than the indifferent destination of a tedious expedition that he finally undertakes ten years later in memory of his now deceased wife. In the eyes of young James Ramsay, the tower represents the goal of a romantic quest: from a distance the lighthouse appeared as "a silvery, misty-looking tower with a yellow eye, that opened suddenly, and softly in the evening."[16] But ten years later, when he has successfully navigated the channel to the island, "the Lighthouse one had seen across the bay all these years; it was a stark tower on a bare rock." The proud tower of spirit, of arrogance, of sexuality, has been reduced to nothing more than an empty structure, devoid of meaning, simply a landmark on the path of life.

Other modernists facing the same dilemma summoned up the same image, perhaps nowhere more appropriately than among the skyscrapers of Manhattan. Book 4 of Malcolm Cowley's *Blue Juniata* (1929), for instance, which gathers the poems that he wrote in 1924–28 following his return from European exile, is entitled simply "The City of Anger." Towers play a conspicuous role in his portrayal of New York, "the metropolis of curiosity and suspicion. . . . the home of lasting impermanence. . . . the seat of violent emotions, hate, desire, envy and contempt."[17] In images echoing *The Waste Land* we see "towers crumbling in the sunshine" ("Ten Good Farms"), while, in a city "cracked open to reveal its secret subways," nothing is visible but a lone man climbing out of the dead crowds and scaling the highest ledges until "the tower bends / like a yellow birch in winter" and hurls its burden into the empty sky ("The Death of Crowds"). The poem "Towers of Song" conjectures that Manhattan was created when "an island uttered incandescent towers, / like frozen simultaneous hymns to Trade." Or, he muses, might a poet have created these "index fingers of infinity," these "towers of intolerable song" simply to "prolong / his furious contempt for sky and sea?" The entire section constitutes an apocalyptic vision of the crumbling towers of civilization.[18]

In an essay entitled "General Aims and Theories" Cowley's contemporary, Hart Crane, addressed the quandary of the contemporary poet forced to operate with the language, images, and myths of a vanished era.

> It is a terrific problem that faces the poet today—a world that is so in transition from a decayed culture toward a reorganization of human evaluations that there are few common terms, general denominators of speech that are solid enough or that ring with any vibration of spiritual conviction. The great mythologies of the past (including the Church) are deprived of enough façade to even launch good raillery against. Yet much of their traditions are [sic] operative still—in millions of chance combinations of related and unrelated detail, psychological reference, figures of speech, precept, etc. These are all a part of our common experience and the terms, at least partially, of that very experience when it defines or extends itself.[19]

In one of his last poems, "The Broken Tower" (1932), Crane exemplified this dilemma through the image of the tower. The poem begins with a survey of the towers of faith from the ziggurats of Babylon to the pagodas, bell towers, and cathedrals of Eastern and Western spirituality:

Oval encyclicals in canyons heaping
The impasse high with choir. Banked voices slain!
Pagodas, campaniles with reveilles outleaping—
O terraced echoes prostrate on the plain! . . .[20]

But the bells have shattered their towers, leaving "the visionary company of love" in a "broken world." The poet's words and blood can no longer sustain the lofty towers of the past. The bell now tolls in his veins, and "the angelus of wars my chest evokes" as the poet "builds, within, a tower that is not stone." Shattered in reality, the tower continues to exist only in the interiorized architecture of the poet's imagination.

◩ 4 ◪

This is not to say that an image so compelling immediately lost its attraction. The modernistic Einsteinturm ("Einstein Tower") in Potsdam, designed by Erich Mendelsohn and dedicated in 1924 as a tribute to the proponent of the general theory of relativity, reifies as an observatory and scientific conference center the ancient Babylonian vision of the tower as a site of astronomy and intellect. Among some conservative writers, even if they did not live in towers, it retained for a time the traditional associations. *The Tower* (*Der Turm*, 1925; revised 1927) is the symbolic title of the tragedy in which the Austrian humanist Hugo von Hofmannsthal sought to illustrate a "conservative revolution" of the sort that he regarded as essential to confront the spiritual decay of modernity[21]—a turn away from what he regarded as the illusory reality of political and social violence to a higher reality of the spirit. Based increasingly loosely (with each successive draft) on Calderón's great baroque play *La vida es sueño*,[22] Hofmannsthal's tragedy relates the story of King Basilius in a legendary seventeenth-century Poland, who learns from a prophecy that his own son is destined to dethrone and humiliate him before the people. When his son Sigismund is born, therefore, Basilius sends him away to be brought up, like Maleine and Axël, in the seclusion of a tower far removed from society and political life. For reasons of his own ambition, the governor of the tower, Julian, educates the prince through the Bible and other books while keeping him cut off from human society. The action begins when twenty-two years have passed and the country has been plunged into chaos by war, inflation, injustice, and corrupt, violent rule; the demoralized populace gathers in the churches to pray for an innocent young king to lead them back to peace and social coherence. At the same time the king's nephew and heir is killed in a hunting accident and his principal adviser, dismayed by the king's corruption, has resigned and withdrawn to a monastery. "The walls are trembling on their very foundations," the king concludes.[23] These events make the king amenable to Julian's suggestion that his son be brought back to court on a trial basis. But the experiment fails: Sigismund, offended by the king's demand that he kill Julian as a conspirator, strikes his father instead and thus fulfills the prophecy.

At this point (the end of act 3) the two principal versions diverge.[24] In the earlier version (1925) Sigismund is sent back to the tower; but Julian stirs up rebellion among the common people, who release Sigismund from his prison. He leads the populace to victory over the forces of violence but is himself killed by treachery at the moment of victory. Nevertheless the forces of decency prevail: it turns out at the very end that Sigismund has merely prepared the way for the true child-king who appears to bring peace and harmony to the land. By 1927, Hofmannsthal was no longer sanguine about his vision of peace: in the second version Sigismund is sentenced by order of the king to be executed; he is rescued at the last minute by the rebellious populace stirred up by Julian; but both he and Julian are killed by a violent demogogue (Hitler?), who seizes power and installs a Sigismund lookalike to assuage the people. The hopeful celebration of the earlier version has given way to a cynical political realism, in which Sigismund remains simply a beacon for the future: "Bear witness that I was here even though no one knew me" are his last words. As Hofmannsthal put it while he was working on the final version: "*Der Turm.* What must be depicted is the true mercilessness of our reality, in which the soul, emerging from a dark mythic realm, gets involved."[25]

Hofmannsthal's shifting views—from his early adaptations of Calderón's play (from 1901 on) through the various versions of *Der Turm* that he wrote and published in the 1920s—are suggested by the very ambiguity of the title-image. (It is not without significance that Hofmannsthal shifted the emphasis, through a change in title, from the metaphysical state of Calderón's *La vida es sueño* to the symbol of *Der Turm.*) The tower emerges initially as an image of absolute power and punishment. But when King Basilius goes to the monastery to consult Brother Ignatius, his former chief minister (act 2), we hear in the background the ominous chant: *Ecce ego suscitabo super Babylonem quasi ventum pestilentem. Et mit-*

tam in Babyloniam ventilatores et ventilabunt eam et demolientur terram eius (Behold, I shall stir up over Babylon a pestilential wind. And I shall send fanners of flame into Babylon and they shall fan it and demolish the land). These words of Jeremiah (condensed from 51.1–2), with their prophecy of the destruction of Babylon for its sins, revive a negative image of the tower: the tower of Babel symbolizing a reign of pride, arrogance, sexual lust, violence. Consistently, when Sigismund lies dying (in the earlier version), believing feverishly that he is back in his tower-prison, he cries out: "Kill the old king! tear down the tower! shatter the chains!" (212)—words that clearly identify the tower as an icon of cruel oppression. At the same time, other passages relate the edifice to the Jungian tower of introspection: for the tower is also "a dark mythic realm" where Sigismund has been preserved from the sins and violence that have corrupted the world outside. In his first encounter with the world his first words (in the final version) to his father are "From whence—so much violence?" (400). And shortly before the end, when the physician has overheard the plot to murder Sigismund, he asks the conspirators: "Who is the judge over purity? Where does innocence finds its judge?" (458). The tower, accordingly, is the preserve of innocence, purity, and spiritual integrity as well as the symbol of violence and pride.[26] But Sigismund has internalized his lessons so well that he has also interiorized the tower. Julian, in his effort to share his ward's newfound political power (act 4), reminds him that he, Julian, led him out of the tower to freedom. Sigismund replies, "Yes, I am [secure], lord and master forever in this fast tower," pointing to his own breast (436). But the tower is not only the proud tower and the tower of introspection; it is also the symbolist

bed with Greek and Latin mottoes, where "the only
ssible life is one of seclusion and study."[32]
Perhaps the most bizarre modern trivialization of the
wer as the locus of sexuality and spirituality was the
ee-story "Tower on the Marsh" erected in 1937 in
wley, Massachusetts, by the then director of the Har-
d Psychological Clinic and his mistress-associate,
nry Murray and Christiana Morgan. Conceived in
cific imitation of the tower at Bollingen—both had
n analyzed and captivated by Jung—and decorated
ide with private symbols and inscriptions carved into
walls, it served for several decades as the (openly se-
t) retreat for the erotic rituals of their "synergic" (=
ulterous) affair, as the site of their "trancing," and as
inspiration for the books and articles that they inces-
tly planned and started (but never actually com-
ted). According to their (utterly unironic) biographer,
lone in their castle, they took on the identities of
na and Mansol and invented laws, contracts, didactic
mulations, rituals, celebrations, and feasts for a multi-
ered fantasy realm—a play world imbued with lusty
ticism."[33] This self-indulgent and ultimately self-de-
uctive couple (she drowned herself in 1967) evidently
ieved that they could achieve Jung's spiritual insights
mimicking the externalities of his life.

◘ 6 ◘

the ancient Babylonian associations of pride, intellect,
d sexuality resonate, finally, in Ayn Rand's *The Foun-
nhead* (1943). It is unnecessary for our purposes to reca-
ulate the plot of the sprawling philosophical novel,

tower, from which the departure leads inevitably to
death. For Sigismund ultimately suffers the same fate as
Maleine and Axël. The ambiguities of Hofmannsthal's
tragedy in its various versions, as exemplified by the different associations of the title-image, have produced a
multiplicity of often conflicting interpretations.[27] The
image of the tower, having loosed itself from specific associations, has become sufficiently multivalent to tolerate
every transformation.

◘ 5 ◘

Woolf may well have been inspired to her essay "The
Leaning Tower" by the example of her friend, Vita Sackville-West, who did in fact inhabit a tower. The gardens
at Sissinghurst Castle are widely known to the public
from the popular garden articles that Sackville-West con-
tributed weekly to the *Observer* from 1947 to 1961. But
the tower photographed in 1942 for a series of articles on
Sissinghurst in *Country Life* was an intensely private
place. Soon after the family moved to Sissinghurst in
1930, Vita claimed the turret-room for her library, and for
the next thirty-two years it remained a sanctuary to which
few were admitted—and then only by invitation. Her
son reported that he had entered the sanctum only three
times during her lifetime.[28] "She filled the room with her
books and personal mementos . . . and as the wallpaper
peeled and faded, and the velvet tassels slowly frayed, she
would never allow them to be renewed. Her possessions
must grow old with her. She must be surrounded by evidence of time."[29] If Sackville-West's earlier works be-
trayed little interest in towers, this translator of Rilke's

Fig. 24. The tower at Sissinghurst Castle.
Permission of Country Life Picture Library.

Elegies from the Castle of Duino (1931) took quickly to her
new surroundings, and the tower soon showed up as the
principal locus of her poetry. In "Sissinghurst" (1930) "a
tired swimmer in the waves of time" sinks "down through
centuries to another clime," where she finds a castle "bur-
ied in time and sleep."

> Here, tall and damask as a summer flower,
> Rise the brick gable and the springing tower;
>   Invading Nature crawls

166

With ivied fingers over rosy wal
. . . .
Holding this myth together un
Anachronistic vagabonds![30]

Yet in this world "where days and y
number" the poet finds nothing mo
tonic solitude and the conventional t
and book. Sackville-West's tower i
ascent of consciousness à la Yeats, fo
of reality in the encounter with Rilk
ber Inhumanist meditations on the
tion, or for Jungian ruminations on tl
personality. The locus of the collecti
almost always conspicuously the "l
tower, to be sure, but what occurs tl
yond the kind of abstruse reading t
tional in British poetic towers from
Shelley to the early Yeats.

> Therefore I'll make of Paracelse
> What time no voice explains an
> Shut out the world, and with a
> Force the reluctant daytime to e
> Prisoned in glass, and circled on
> One ring of light within these d
> Therefore within my secret roon
> While others sleep, and call on I
> By few short centuries removed

Symptomatically, when Sackville-W
taigne's tower in 1954, she was "entra
band noted in his diaries, by the stu

which traces the career of the brilliant architect Howard
Roark from the point at which he is expelled from architecture school for his refusal to accept the prevailing
norms, to the culmination, when he blows up a federal
housing project he has designed rather than allow his
conception to be spoiled by mediocre tamperers. At his
trial Roark expounds his (and Rand's) theory of heroic
individualism as opposed to the mindless collectivism
that he sees destroying Western civilization.

> The first right on earth is the right of the ego. Man's
> first duty is to himself. His moral law is never to place
> his prime goal within the persons of others. His moral
> obligation is to do what he wishes, provided his wish
> does not depend *primarily* upon other men. This in-
> cludes the whole sphere of his creative faculty, his
> thinking, his work.[34]

What matters in our context is the role that towers, in the
form of skyscrapers, play in the novel as the symbol for
Rand's overreachers. All three of the central characters are
obsessed by them and their ancient associations. Following his expulsion from the Stanton Institute of Technology, Roark goes to work for the renegade architect Henry
Cameron, who is described as having been one of the
earliest designers to understand the "new miracle" of the
skyscraper. "He was among the first and the few who
accepted the truth that a tall building must look tall. . . .
[and] must not copy the Greeks" (44–45). When Roark
opens his first office, it is situated on the top of an old
building, and years later the same impulse leads him to
move his office to the top floor of a skyscraper he has
designed, from whose heights he can look down at the
whole of Manhattan.

If the tower is associated in Roark's mind with the intellectual power of titanic creators, it has additional meanings for other characters. When Roark's lover, Dominique Francon, meets the newspaper tycoon Gail Wynand, she confesses to him that she has received "that particular sense of sacred rapture men say they experience in contemplating nature" only from skyscrapers (447). Sexuality and seclusion—virtually that of the sacred priestess—prevail following their marriage when, for two weeks, they never leave their penthouse fifty-seven floors above the city. Dominique could easily have descended by elevator to the city below, but "She had no desire to resist, to wonder, to question. It was enchantment and peace" (487). Later Wynand reminds her, as they stand looking down at the city, that the skyscrapers were "the first link between us" (499). "What we love about these buildings, Dominique, is the creative faculty, the heroic in man."

Toward the end of the novel, when Wynand commissions Roark to construct the Wynand Building as a monument to his sense of power, he tells the architect that he wants it to be "the tallest structure of the city" (692). Wynand believes that "The age of the skyscraper is gone. This is the age of the housing project. Which is always a prelude to the age of the cave" (693). He intends his building to be "a gesture against the whole world. . . . The last achievement of man on earth before mankind destroys itself." Fittingly, on the last page of the novel, when Dominique goes to meet Roark, for whom she has left Wynand, she seeks him out on the top platform of the new skyscraper under construction. As she rises on the hoist, the other skyscrapers of the city are left far below. "Then there was only the ocean and the sky and the figure of Howard Roark." It is difficult to imagine a contemporary work that recapitulates more consistently the ancient tower-associations of power, pride, intellect, and sexuality.

□ 7 □

The era of poetic towers ended abruptly with World War II, which demonstrated with ruthless efficiency that even the sturdiest tower cannot provide a sanctuary against the weapons of technology. (The Kaiser Wilhelm Memorial Church, with its bombed-out tower, is maintained in the heart of Berlin as a vivid reminder of the horrors of war.) This is evident in Thomas Bernhard's prize-winning novella *Amras* (1964), where the tower is transformed into the scene of death and madness.[35] Following the suicide of their parents—their father has squandered the fortune of a distinguished old Tirolese family—two brothers are sequestered by their uncle in a tower (the landmark tower of Amras, near Innsbruck) allegedly to protect them from the curious or malevolent actions of others. It is explained that they were also involved in the suicide pact but survived; only their uncle's influence can protect them from a law condemning attempted suicides to the madhouse. The work by the younger Austrian displays certain implicit similarities with Hofmannsthal's *The Tower*[36]—notably the implication that the young men, themselves linked in a homoerotic relationship, are being put away to prevent them from discovering that their uncle has somehow cheated them out of their rightful inheritance. Like Sigismund, both the narrator and his brother perish: the one through a suicidal plunge from the tower, the other through his confinement in a madhouse. But there is no redeeming vision. The tower, initially perceived as a traditional place of security and refuge from the world, turns out during the two and a half months of their sojourn to be also an image of consciousness, the terrible consciousness that leads to madness and death. "In the tower we had suddenly become fully aware of the darkest aspects of being, . . . in the tower we had become conscious of ourselves, we looked at ourselves, for the first time, from without *and* within" (34).

The devalued tower did not simply disappear from the cultural horizon. Like other archetypal images that have outlived their day, it was transformed into an institution—or into parody. The towers inhabited by Rilke and Jung still remain in family possession. Thoor Ballylee was converted in 1965 into a national monument, visited reverently by Yeats's admirers. And the town of Carmel prides itself on its famous resident, whose Hawk Tower is now maintained as a tourist attraction by the Tor House Foundation.

As for parody, Woody Allen's story "The Irish Genius" is supposed to be a review of *The Annotated Poems of Sean O'Shawn*, an Irish poet who amounts to an amalgam of Joyce and Yeats. The sample nonsense verse that the author quotes is entitled "Beyond Ichor" and begins:

> Let us sail. Sail with
> Fogarty's chin to Alexandria,
> While the Beamish Brothers
> Hurry giggling to the tower. . . .[37]

A note explains that O'Shawn lived in a low tower (only six feet high) just south of Dublin with Harry O'Connel, a friend with literary pretensions. Parody, of course, de-

Fig. 25. Prayer tower at Oral Roberts University, Tulsa, Oklahoma. Courtesy of Oral Roberts University.

pends upon recognition. The fact that Allen counts on a laugh from his allusion to the tower attests to the familiarity of the image in literature of the twentieth century.

As a final example let us consider the two-hundred-foot-high prayer tower erected in 1967 on the campus of Oral Roberts University in Tulsa, Oklahoma. Prayer towers stand conspicuously in a tradition that extends back by way of Luther's tower in Wittenberg and the Gothic cathedrals to the great Mesopotamian ziggurats at the beginning of history. The prayer tower of the south-western interdenominational Christian university, a stunning spiral culminating in an eternal flame and marking symbolically the center of the campus, is clearly indebted to this venerable heritage. Serving as a visitors' center, it also houses a forty-person ministry that responds with prayer to some fifty thousand phone and Internet requests per month. But Reverend Roberts's use of the tower also displays a shrewd calculation that owes as much to Elmer Gantry as to the priests of Etemenanki. In January 1987 Mr. Roberts announced to viewers of his weekly television program that he expected to die if he failed to meet an $8 million fund-raising goal by the end of March. "I am going to be in and out of the prayer tower praying and fasting until victory comes or God calls me home."[38] I leave it to readers who have followed this cultural history of towers to decide for themselves whether the prayer tower in Oklahoma amounts to renewal, institutionalization, or parody of the ancient image—or a postmodern mélange of all three.

NOTES

CHAPTER ONE
THE PROUD TOWERS

1. Joseph Campbell, *The Mythic Image* (Princeton, NJ: Princeton University Press, 1974), 76.

2. Tamara M. Green, "Towers," in *The Encyclopedia of Religion*, ed. Mircea Eliade, vol. 14 (New York: Macmillan, 1987), 583–84.

3. Magda Révesz-Alexander, *Der Turm als Symbol und Erlebnis* (The Hague: Nijhoff, 1953), 7–8.

4. Evelyn Klengel-Brandt, *Der Turm von Babylon: Legende und Geschichte eines Bauwerkes* (Vienna: Anton Schroll, 1982), 152–54.

5. Ibid., 52–56.

6. Campbell, *The Mythic Image*, 87.

7. Klengel-Brandt, *Der Turm von Babylon*, 74–93; see also Erwin Heinle and Fritz Leonhardt, *Towers: A Historical Survey*, trans. Martha Humphreys (New York: Rizzoli, 1989), 26–30.

8. S. R. Driver, *The Book of Genesis with Introduction and Notes*, 12th ed. (London: Methuen, 1926), 132–37.

9. For other implications, see Leon R. Cass, "What's Wrong with Babel?" *American Scholar* 58 (1989): 41–60.

10. Heinle and Leonhardt, *Towers*, 36; and Günter Meissner and Heinz Bronowski, *Towers and Turrets of Europe*, trans. C.X.V. Salt (Erfurt: Edition Leipzig, 1974), 9.

11. Révesz-Alexander, *Der Turm*, 128.

12. Heinle and Leonhardt, *Towers*, 32–35.

13. Ibid., 10, 24.

14. Meissner and Bronowski, *Towers and Turrets of Europe*, 29.

15. Heinle and Leonhardt, *Towers*, 48–83.

16. Manfred Lurker, *Wörterbuch biblischer Bilder und Symbole* (Munich: Kösel, 1973), 331.

17. Meissner and Bronowski, *Towers and Turrets of Europe*, 12.

18. Wolfgang Beeh, "Zur Bedeutungsgeschichte des Turmes: Der Kapellenturm in Rottweil," *Jahrbuch für Ästhetik und allgemeine Kunstwissenschaft* 6 (1961): 177–206; here 184–86.

19. Ibid., 193–201.

20. Heinle and Leonhardt, *Towers*, 12.

21. Helmut Minkowski, *Vermutungen über den Turm zu Babel* (Freren: Luca, 1991), provides rich documentation and reproductions of works throughout history, but especially from the century 1550–1650.

22. Raimond van Marle, *Iconographie de l'art profane au moyen-âge et à la renaissance et la décoration des demeures*, 2 vols. (The Hague: Nijhoff, 1932), 2:244 (fig. 272).

23. "De trois commerces" (bk. 3, chap. 3), in Montaigne, *Essais*, ed. Maurice Rat, vol. 3 (Paris: Garnier, 1965), 45.

24. Robert Burton, *The Anatomy of Melancholy*, ed. A. R. Shilleto, vol. 1 (London: Bell, 1903), 14.

25. Lurker, *Wörterbuch biblischer Bilder und Symbole*, 331.

26. Katarzyna Murawska, "An Image of Mysterious Wisdom Won by Toil: The Tower as Symbol of Thoughtful Isolation in English Art and Literature from Milton to Yeats," *artibus et historiae* 3 (1982): 141–62.

27. Edmund Burke, *A Philosophical Enquiry into the Origin of Our Ideas of the Sublime and Beautiful*, ed. James T. Boulton (London: Routledge, 1958), 72.

28. Warren Hunting Smith, *Architecture in English Fiction* (New Haven: Yale University Press, 1934), 8–9, 15–17, 110–15.

29. David Perkins, *The Quest for Permanence: The Symbolism of Wordsworth, Shelley and Keats* (Cambridge: Harvard University Press, 1959), 185.

30. Stephen Gilman, *The Tower as Emblem: Chapters VIII, IX and XX of the Chartreuse de Parme*, Analecta Romanica 22 (Frankfurt am Main: Klostermann, 1967).

31. Annette von Droste-Hülshoff, *Sämtliche Werke*, ed. Clemens Heselhaus (Munich: Hanser, 1966), 124–25.

32. Edgar Allan Poe, *Selected Poetry and Prose*, ed. T. O. Mabbott (New York: Modern Library, 1951), 409.

33. Herman Melville, *Billy Budd and Other Tales*, with an afterword by Willard Thorp (New York: Penguin/Signet Classics, 1979), 283–97; here 284.

34. Maurice Beebe, *Ivory Towers and Sacred Founts: The Artist as Hero in Fiction from Goethe to Joyce* (New York: New York University Press, 1964), is concerned, as his subtitle indicates, not with actual towers but with the metaphorical tradition that exalts art above life.

35. Robert Finch, "Ivory Tower," *University of Toronto Quarterly* 25 (1955): 23–37; here 36.

36. Charles-Augustin Sainte-Beuve, *Poésies complètes*, vol. 2 (Paris: Michel Lévy, 1863), 231.

37. Erwin Panofsky, "In Defense of the Ivory Tower," *APGA. Report of the Third Conference held at the Graduate College of Princeton University on Jan. 1–3, 1953*; reprinted in *Journal of the American Institute of Architects* 32 (July 1959): 19 ff.

38. Rolf Bergmann, "Der elfenbeinerne Turm in der deutschen Literatur," *Zeitschrift für deutsches Altertum und deutsche Literatur* 92 (1963/64): 292–320.

39. Cited in ibid., 305.

40. Robert Browning, *Poetical Works 1833–1864*, ed. Ian Jack (London: Oxford University Press, 1970).

41. Friedrich Nietzsche, *Werke und Briefe*, Historisch-Kritische Gesamtausgabe, vol. 1: *Jugendschriften 1854–1861*, ed. Hans Joachim Mette (Munich: Beck, 1983), 54–55.

42. Philippe-Auguste Villiers de l'Isle-Adam, *Oeuvres complètes*, vol. 4 (Paris: Mercure de France, 1914–31).

43. *Handbook of Russian Literature*, ed. Victor Terras (New Haven: Yale University Press, 1985), 205, 462.

44. André Gide, *Romans, récits et soties. Oeuvres lyriques* (Paris: Gallimard, 1958), 94.

45. For other examples of metaphorical usage in such disparate fields as politics and academic life, see Bergmann, "Der elfenbeinerne Turm."

46. See in this connection Hermann J. Weigand, *The Modern Ibsen: A Reconsideration* (1925; reprint, New York: Dutton, 1960), 274–309; and Jan Kott, "Ibsen Read Anew," in his *The Theater of Essence and Other Essays* (Evanston, IL: Northwestern University Press, 1984), 31–60; esp. 49–54.

47. Quoted by Thomas A. P. van Leeuwen, *The Skyward Trend of Thought: The Metaphysics of the American Skyscraper* (Cambridge: MIT Press, 1988), 39.

48. Ibid., 41. The following examples are taken from pages 12–13, 34, 60, and 69.

49. Archibald MacLeish, *Tower of Ivory* (New Haven: Yale University Press, 1917).

50. Henry James, *The Ivory Tower* (New York: Scribner, 1945), 147, 214–15.

51. See Percy Lubbock's preface to the New York Edition, v.

CHAPER TWO
WILLIAM BUTLER YEATS

1. David Pierce, *Yeats's Worlds: Ireland, England and the Poetic Imagination* (New Haven and London: Yale University Press, 1995), 183–91.

2. I cite the poems according to *The Collected Poems of W. B. Yeats*, Definitive Edition (New York: Macmillan, 1959).

3. Letter of 23 May 1916 to John Quinn; *The Letters of W. B. Yeats*, ed. Allan Wade (London: Rupert Hart-Davis, 1954), 614.

4. "A People's Theatre," in *Plays and Controversies* (New York: Macmillan, 1924), 215.

5. Mary Hanley and Liam Miller, *Thoor Ballylee: Home of William Butler Yeats*, 3d ed. (Gerards Cross, Buckinghamshire: Colin Smythe, 1995), 10–11.

6. First published in *The Dome* (1899), it was later included in the second edition of *The Celtic Twilight* (1902) and reprinted in *Mythologies* (London: Macmillan, 1959), 22–30; here 22.

7. Letter of April 1922 to Olivia Shakespear; *Letters*, 680.

8. Letter of 12 May 1917 to his father; *Letters*, 624.

9. Hanley and Miller, *Thoor Ballylee*, 13–14.

10. Letter of 23 July 1918 to John Quinn; *Letters*, 651.

11. Ibid. This early draft contains details lacking in the version subsequently published as the last poem of *Michael Robartes and the Dancer* (1921).

12. Frank Tuohy, *Yeats* (London: Macmillan, 1976), 172.

13. W. B. Yeats, *Essays and Introductions* (New York: Macmillan, 1961), 87.

14. "The Philosophy of Shelley's Poetry" (1900), in *Essays and Introductions*, 87.

15. "Discoveries" (1906), in *Essays and Introductions*, 294.

16. "The Trembling of the Veil" (1922), in *The Autobiography of W. B. Yeats* (New York: Macmillan, 1953), 105.

17. Epilogue to *Per Amica Silentia Lunae*; reprinted in *Mythologies*, 367.

18. A. Norman Jeffares, "Thoor, Ballylee," *English Studies* 28 (1947): 161–68; here 163. See also Jeffares, *W. B. Yeats: Man and Poet*, 2d ed. (London: Routledge and Kegan Paul, 1962), 214–20.

19. "Discoveries," in *Essays and Introductions*, 290–91.

20. *Autobiography*, 101: "I was full of thought, often very abstract thought, longing all the while to be full of images, because I had gone to the art school instead of a university."

21. Hugh Kenner, "The Sacred Book of the Arts," in *Yeats: A Collection of Critical Essays*, ed. John Unterecker (Englewood Cliffs, NJ: Prentice-Hall, 1963), 10–22; here 22.

22. Letter of 23 July 1918 to John Quinn; *Letters*, 651.

23. Letter of 11 July 1919 to John Quinn; *Letters*, 659.

24. Edward Bruce Westbrook, "The Tower Symbol in the Poetry of William Butler Yeats" (Ph.D. diss., University of North Carolina, 1972), 79. But I cannot agree with Westbrook, 4, that the tower represented Irish nationalism even in Yeats's earliest thought; or, 81, that by 1919 the tower had already assumed cosmic symbolism.

25. Letter of 11 July 1919 to John Quinn; *Letters*, 659.

26. Letter of 6 September 1921; *W. B. Yeats and T. Sturge Moore: Their Correspondence 1901–1937*, ed. Ursula Bridge (London: Routledge and Kegan Paul, 1953), 38.

27. Jeanette Lander, *William Butler Yeats. Die Bildersprache seiner Lyrik* (Stuttgart: Kohlhammer, 1967), 82 ff., considers the tower only as part of a larger complex of images embracing the adjacent bridge and river.

28. The importance of the tower in Yeats's thought and poetry has of course not gone unremarked. See Jeffares, "Thoor, Ballylee"; T. R. Henn, *The Lonely Tower: Studies in the Poetry of W. B. Yeats*, 2d ed. (London: Methuen, 1965), 13–14, 131–34; John Unterecker, *A Reader's Guide to William Butler Yeats* (New York: Noonday, 1959); A. Norman Jeffares, *A Commentary on the Collected Poems of W. B. Yeats* (Stanford: Stanford University Press, 1968); and especially Westbrook's dissertation, "The Tower Symbol." Only Westbrook looks for a pattern of development rather than a static image. My own reading, while coinciding in many respects with Westbrook's, differs in certain crucial points of interpretation and, hence, of development. Specifically, I see a much greater symbolic consistency in Yeats's shifting physical propinquity to the tower.

29. The parallels between the two volumes—evident in the corresponding poems "Sailing to Byzantium" and "Byzantium," in the parallel sequences "A Man Young and Old" and "A Woman Young and Old," in the adaptations of Sophocles (from *Oedipus* and *Antigone*), and in the contrasting images (sterility vs. regeneration, masculine vs. feminine, political vs. aesthetic)—have been extensively analyzed. See Unterecker, *A Reader's Guide*, 169–70; and Eitel Timm, *W. B. Yeats*, Erträge der Forschung 251 (Darmstadt: Wissenschaftliche Buchgesellschaft, 13–14, 130–31. For an evaluative synthesis of critical opinion on the two volumes, see Timm, 117–41.

30. Letter of 27 July 1922 to Olivia Shakespear; *Letters*, 688.

31. Letter of April 1922 to Olivia Shakespear; *Letters*, 680.

32. Letter of 25 April 1928 to Olivia Shakespear; *Letters*, 742.

33. Letter of April 1922 to Olivia Shakespear; *Letters*, 680.

34. Here I disagree with Westbrook, "The Tower Symbol," 103–4, who in his otherwise plausible reading of this poem equates the empty nest with a "heart fed on false values and fantasies" and fails to note the traditional symbolism of the bees.

35. On Yeats's re-creation of history in "The Tower," see esp. Thomas R. Whitaker, *Swan and Shadow: Yeats's Dialogue with History* (Chapel Hill: University of North Carolina Press, 1964), 194–203.

36. Letter of 21 September 1927 to Sturge Moore; *Correspondence*, 113.

37. Denis Donoghue, "On 'The Winding Stair,' " in *An Honoured Guest: New Essays on W. B. Yeats*, ed. Denis Donoghue and J. R. Mulryne (London: Edward Arnold, 1965), 102–23, argues that it is the basic pattern of the book to acknowledge antinomies, only to subvert them whenever possible (112). Donoghue expands his discussion of consciousness as conflict, which he terms "the most important article in Yeats's faith as a poet," in his book *William Butler Yeats* (New York: Ecco, 1971), 34–69. Here I agree with Donoghue against those critics (Ellmann, Westbrook) who emphasize the negative side of the tower—its incompleteness, its despair.

38. Letter of July/August 1927 to Olivia Shakespear; *Letters*, 727.

39. Yeats's antidemocratic leanings have been thoroughly discussed. See Donoghue, *William Butler Yeats*, 126–46; Elizabeth Cullingford, *Yeats, Ireland, and Fascism* (London: Macmillan, 1981); and Grattan Freyer, *W. B. Yeats and the Anti-Democratic Tradition* (Dublin: Gill and Macmillan, 1981).

40. Westbrook, "The Tower Symbol," 122–28, offers a thorough discussion of Yeats's Anglo-Irish quadruples.

41. Westbrook (ibid., 158–59) stresses this shift from Soul to Self.

42. See the extensive interpretation of this poem in Edward Engelberg, *The Vast Design: Patterns in W. B. Yeats's Aesthetic* (Toronto: University of Toronto Press, 1964), 180–204—one of the rare studies seeking to locate Yeats in a comparative European, rather than a narrowly English, context.

43. Unterecker, *A Reader's Guide*, 292–93; Jon Stallworthy, *Between the Lines: Yeats's Poetry in the Making* (Oxford: Clarendon, 1963), 222–42; Henn, *The Lonely Tower*, 238–39. In contrast to these positive interpretations, J. R. Mulryne, "The 'Last Poems,' " in *An Honoured Guest*, 124–42, argues that the Black Tower is no longer a path to wisdom but only a place of refuge, while Westbrook, "The Tower Symbol," 179, believes that the men of the tower are no more than "simple-minded fanatics."

44. W. B. Yeats, *Explorations* (New York: Macmillan 1962), 337.

CHAPTER THREE
ROBINSON JEFFERS

1. Letter of 4 March 1931 to Babette Deutsch; in *The Selected Letters of Robinson Jeffers, 1897–1962*, ed. Ann N. Ridgeway (Baltimore: Johns Hopkins University Press, 1968), 179. Years later Jeffers recalled a subsequent visit to Yeats's tower: "We climbed the winding stair of the old Norman tower; every window had been broken, every corner was full of filth and broken bottles. Una notes in her diary, 'I shall never come here again. It is too sad.' It was the end of an epoch." In Jeffers's foreword to Una Jeffers, *Visits to Ireland: Travel Diaries of Una Jeffers* (Los Angeles: Ward Ritchie Press, 1954).

2. Letter of 31 August 1929 to Albert Bender; *Letters*, 155.

3. Letter of 20 December 1929 to Albert Bender; *Letters*, 164.

4. For a survey of the fluctuating reception of Jeffers's works, see Alex A. Vardamis, *The Critical Reputation of Robinson Jeffers: A Bibliographical Study* (Hamden, CT: Archon Books, 1972).

5. *The Selected Poetry of Robinson Jeffers* (New York: Random House, 1938), xv.

6. For biographical details I have followed chiefly Melba Berry Bennett, *The Stone Mason of Tor House: The Life and Work of Robinson Jeffers* (Los Angeles: Ward Ritchie Press, 1966); and James Karman, *Robinson Jeffers: Poet of California* (San Francisco: Chronicle Books, 1987).

7. Karman, *Jeffers: Poet of California*, 25.

8. *Selected Poetry*, xv–xvi.

9. Karman: *Jeffers: Poet of California*, 28.

10. Bennett, *The Stone Mason*, 87.

11. Jeffers's poems are cited here and elsewhere according to the three-volume edition of *The Collected Poetry of Robinson Jeffers*, ed. Tim Hunt (Stanford: Stanford University Press, 1988, 1989, 1991).

12. Jeffers noted that "I have had two or three of his odes in my memory for thirty years, and still say them to myself for pleasure in the sound of the verses and their flawless architecture." Cited by Bennett, *The Stone Mason*, 89. It is not unlikely that one of those odes was 3.30 with its famous first line hailing the eternity of poetry that is more lasting even than bronze: *exegi monumentum aere perennius*.

13. *Selected Poetry*, xiv.

14. Letter of 23 April 1934 to Lawrence Clark Powell; *Letters*, 213.

15. Letter of 10 November 1927; *Letters*, 126.

16. *Letters*, 138.

17. Ibid., 170.

18. Ibid., 129.

19. Ibid., 353.

20. Donnan Jeffers, "Some Notes on the Building of Tor House," *The Robinson Jeffers Newsletter: A Jubilee Gathering, 1962–1988*, ed. Robert J. Brophy (Los Angeles: Occidental College, 1988), 111–25; here 118.

21. Bennett, *The Stone Mason*, 102.

22. Karman, *Jeffers: Poet of California*, 111.

23. Robert J. Brophy, "The Tor House Library: Jeffers' Books," in *The Robinson Jeffers Newsletter: A Jubilee Gathering 1962–1988*, 19.

24. Bennett, *The Stone Mason*, 101.

25. Letter of 1924 to George Sterling; *Letters*, 29.

26. Letter of 11 February 1925 to Maurice Browne; *Letters*, 33. The passage, from Eclogues 8.108, wonders "whether those who love create their own dreams."

27. Karman, *Jeffers: Poet of California*, 91.

28. Letter of 10 November 1927 to Benjamin De Casseres; *Letters*, 126; and Bennett, *The Stone Mason*, 100–101.

29. Donnan Jeffers, "Some Notes on the Building of Tor House," 125.

30. Bennett, *The Stone Mason*, 40.

31. Letter of 9 November 1932 to Jeremy Ingalls; *Letters*, 200.

32. *New York Times Magazine*, 18 January 1948; reprinted in Bennett, *The Stone Mason*, 202–207; here 206.

33. *Letters*, 201. Lucretius also occurs in the poems: e.g., "Prescription of Painful Ends" (in *Be Angry at the Sun*); or "De Rerum Virtute" (in *Hungerfield*) with its titular allusion to *De rerum natura*.

34. Letter of 17 May 1935 to Louis Adamic; *Letters*, 226.

35. The fact did not go unremarked by a hostile press. Ruth Lechlitner, in her review of *Solstice and Other Poems* in *New Republic* 85 (8 January 1936): 262, observed tartly: "Not that he desires fascism or communism either— oh no. Just plain annihilation of humankind (followed by peace) will do Mr. Jeffers nicely. Provided, I gather, that he can sit alone in his stone tower, surrounded by California scenery, while the whole disgusting business is going on, and dash off a last poem or two before Peace gathers him to her bosom."

36. Cited by Frederic I. Carpenter, *Robinson Jeffers* (New York: Twayne, 1962), 69.

37. See the conspicuously sympathetic discussion of Jeffers (by various hands) in *Kindlers Neues Literatur Lexikon*, ed. Walter Jens, vol. 8 (Munich: Kindler, 1990), 695–706.

38. *Letters*, 335 n. 3.

39. *Selected Poetry*, xvii.

40. This identification was noted by critics, who sometimes made the analogy in their reviews: e.g., David Littlejohn, "Cassandra Grown Tired," *Commonweal* 79 (7 December 1962): 276–78.

41. Carpenter, *Robinson Jeffers*, 69.

42. For a discussion of Aeschylus's trilogy, especially in its legal dimensions, see Theodore Ziolkowski, *The Mirror of Justice: Literary Reflections of Legal Crises* (Princeton, NJ: Princeton University Press, 1997), 20–41.

43. For interpretations of the play see Carpenter, *Robinson Jeffers*, 69–72; Robert J. Brophy, *Robinson Jeffers: Myth, Ritual, and Symbol in His Narrative Poems* (Cleveland and London: Case Western Reserve University Press, 1973), 113–58 (based mainly on Joseph Campbell, Northrop Frye, and Mircea Eliade); the Freudian reading by Robert Zaller, *The Cliffs of Solitude: A Reading of Robinson Jeffers* (Cambridge: Cambridge University Press, 1983), 23–36; and William H. Nolte, *Rock and Hawk: Robinson Jeffers and the Romantic Agony* (Athens: University of Georgia Press, 1978), 117–20.

44. Letter of 18 March 1925; *Letters*, 35.

45. Letter of November 1929 to Rudolph Gilbert; *Letters*, 159.

46. Brophy, *Robinson Jeffers: Myth, Ritual, and Symbol*, 123.

47. Letter of 18 March 1925; *Letters*, 35.

48. Letter of 14 December 1928; *Letters*, 138.

49. *The Double Axe and Other Poems* (New York: Random House, 1948), vii. This preface is not included in *The Collected Poetry*.

Chapter Four
Rainer Maria Rilke

1. *Rainer Maria Rilke: A Verse Concordance to His Complete Lyrical Poetry*, ed. Ulrich K. Goldsmith et al. (Leeds: W. S. Maney, 1980).

2. "Zwei Prager Geschichten"; Rilke's works are cited, if not otherwise indicated, by volume and page from the six-volume *Sämtliche Werke*, ed. Ernst Zinn (Frankfurt am Main: Insel, 1955–66); here 4:131.

3. Because Rilke suppressed his first book of poems, *Life and Songs* (*Leben und Lieder*, 1894), *Larenopfer* actually comprises the first poems in his collected poetry.

4. In a letter of 11 November 1900 to Paula Becker; in *Briefe und Tagebücher aus der Frühzeit, 1899 bis 1902*, ed. Ruth Sieber-Rilke and Carl Sieber (Leipzig: Insel, 1933), 72.

5. *Florenzer Tagebuch*; in *Tagebücher aus der Frühzeit*, ed. Ruth Sieber-Rilke and Carl Sieber (Frankfurt am Main: Insel, 1973), 19.

6. Letter of 20 April [2 May] 1899 to Jelena M. Woronina; in *Rilke und Russland. Briefe, Erinnerungen, Gedichte*, ed. Konstantin Asodowski (Frankfurt am Main: Insel, 1986), 87.

7. Letter of 5 March 1902 to Alexej S. Suworin; *Rilke und Russland*, 337.

8. Letter of 25 January 1906 to Clara Rilke; in Rainer Maria Rilke, *Briefe*, ed. Ruth Sieber-Rilke and Karl Altheim (Wiesbaden: Insel, 1950), 115. All letters are cited from this edition unless otherwise indicated.

9. Letter of 8 August 1903 to Lou Andreas-Salomé; *Briefe*, 58: "Das Ding ist bestimmt, das Kunst-Ding muß noch bestimmter sein; von allem Zufall fortgenommen, jeder Unklarheit entrückt, der Zeit enthoben und dem Raum gegeben, ist es dauernd geworden, fähig zur Ewigkeit."

10. Rilke reported the death of the bell-ringer in a letter of 20 August 1908 to Mathilde Vollmoeller; cited by H. Uyttersprot, "R. M. Rilke: Der Turm," *Neophilologus* 39 (1955): 262–75.

11. Heidi Heimann, " 'O wenn er steigt, behangen wie ein Stier.' Rilkes Gedicht 'Der Turm,' " *Publications of the English Goethe Society* 32 (1961–62): 46–73, suggests that the reference here is to Orpheus, laden with his lyre, whose ascent from the underworld Rilke had earlier (1904) portrayed in the great poem "Orpheus. Eurydike. Hermes." But I am not persuaded by her interpretation and prefer the less far-fetched one (*er = der Abgrund*) suggested by Uyttersprot and by Herbert W. Belmore in his response to Heimann's article; "Eine Entgegnung," *Publications of the English Goethe Society* 33 (1962–63): 1–5.

12. Brigitte L. Bradley, *R. M. Rilkes Neue Gedichte. Ihr zyklisches Gefüge* (Bern and Munich: Francke, 1967), 135–37.

13. Rilke used this device—the reification of a metaphor—much more successfully in his poem "Ausgesetzt auf den Bergen des Herzens" (1914; 2:94–95).

14. Letter of 27 October 1915 to Ellen Delp; *Briefe*, 509.

15. Letter of 8 November 1915 to Lotte Hepner; *Briefe*, 510–16; here 516: "eine großartig durchdrungene Angst, . . . eine Fuge von Angst gleichsam, ein riesiger Bau, ein Angst-Turm mit Gängen und Treppen und geländerlosen Vorsprüngen und Abstürzen nach allen Seiten."

16. See the discussion of this work in Theodore Ziolkowski, *Dimensions of the Modern Novel* (Princeton, NJ: Princeton University Press, 1969), 3–36.

17. Ralph Freedman, *Life of a Poet: Rainer Maria Rilke* (New York: Farrar, Straus and Giroux, 1996), 401, suggests that "the idea of hymns to the rising phallus had been with Rilke for years—beginning with dis-

cussions with Lou [Andreas-Salomé] after the Psychoanalytic Congress in 1913."

18. Klaus Kanzog, "Wortbildwahl und phallisches Motiv bei R. M. Rilke. Beitrag zu einem zukünftigen Rilke-Wörterbuch," *Zeitschrift für deutsche Philologie* 76 (1957): 203–28. In his useful piece, which catalogs many of the passages used in my analysis, Kanzog surprisingly does not mention this perhaps most phallic of Rilke's poems.

19. Letter of 26 June 1904 to Clara Rilke; *Briefe*, 82.

20. Letter of 23 October 1909; in R. M. Rilke, *Briefe an seinen Verleger, 1906–1926*, ed. Ruth Sieber-Rilke and Carl Sieber, 2d ed., vol. 1 (Wiesbaden: Insel, 1949), 179.

21. Letter of 25 November 1911 to Hedwig Fischer; *Briefe*, 294.

22. Letter of 30 November 1916; in Rainer Maria Rilke and Marie von Thurn und Taxis, *Briefwechsel*, ed. Ernst Zinn, vol. 2 (Zurich: Niehans, 1951), 498.

23. Letter of 4 July 1921; in R. M. Rilke, *Briefe an Nanny Wunderly-Volkart*, ed. Niklaus Bigler and Rätus Luck, vol. 1 (Frankfurt am Main: Insel, 1977), 496–98. See the account of these years in J. R. von Salis, *Rainer Maria Rilkes Schweizer Jahre: Ein Beitrag zur Biographie von Rilkes Spätzeit*, 3d ed. (Frauenfeld: Huber, 1952), 94–105.

24. Letter of 9 July 1921; *Briefe an Nanny Wunderly-Volkart*, 505.

25. Letter of 25 July 1921; *Briefe*, 677–82.

26. Letter of 27 July 1921; *Briefe an Nanny Wunderly-Volkart*, 526.

27. Letter of 17 August 1921 to Nora Purtscher-Wydenbruck; *Briefe*, 687–88.

28. Letter of 29 December 1921 to Lou Andreas-Salomé; in *Briefe aus Muzot, 1921 bis 1926*, ed. Ruth Sieber-Rilke and Carl Sieber (Leipzig: Insel, 1935), 72, 74.

29. Letter of 9 February 1922 to Anton Kippenberg; *Briefe*, 741.

30. R. M. Rilke and Merline, *Correspondence 1920–1926*, ed. Dieter Bassermann (Zurich: Niehans, 1954), 393. And the same expression recurs in a letter of 11 February to Lou Andreas Salomé; *Briefe*, 744.

31. *Briefe*, 742.

32. Ibid., 743.

33. See in this connection, and for a full analysis of the cycle, Theodore Ziolkowski, *The Classical German Elegy, 1795–1950* (Princeton, NJ: Princeton University Press, 1980).

34. Letter of 13 November 1925 to Witold Hulewicz; *Briefe*, 900.

35. Letter of 15 April 1924 to Baronin Ledebur; *Briefe aus Muzot*, 264.

36. Letter of 18 December 1925 to Arthur Fischer-Colbrie; *Briefe aus Muzot*, 346.

37. Letter of 27 February 1926 to Inga Junghanns; *Briefe aus Muzot*, 356.

38. On Rilke's response to the political and social turmoil of the period see especially R. M. Rilke, *Briefe zur Politik*, ed. Joachim W. Storck (Frankfurt am Main and Leipzig: Insel, 1992).

39. Letter of 15 July 1922 to Margot Gräfin Sizzo-Noris-Crouy; *Briefe zur Politik*, 393.

40. Letter of 25 July 1921; *Briefe an Nanny Wunderly-Volkart*, 520.

CHAPTER FIVE
CARL GUSTAV JUNG

1. *Erinnerungen, Träume, Gedanken von C. G. Jung*, aufgezeichnet und herausgegeben von Aniela Jaffé (Zurich and Stuttgart: Rascher, 1962); *Memories, Dreams, Reflections*, trans. Richard and Clara Winston (New York: Random House/Vintage, 1963). I cite the text from the English translation except for the occasional cases when the translation obscures or omits a passage in the German original (*ETG*).

2. I refer throughout to the Bollingen Edition of Jung's Collected Works as published by Princeton University Press.

3. *C. G. Jung. Wort und Bild*, ed. Aniela Jaffé (Olten and Freiburg im Breisgau: Walter, 1977); trans. Krishna Winston, *C. G. Jung: Word and Image*, Bollingen Series 97:2 (Princeton, NJ: Princeton University Press, 1979), 140–41. I quote the translation with occasional emendations.

4. "Mind and Earth," in *Civilization in Transition*, trans. R.F.C. Hull, 2d ed. (Princeton, NJ: Princeton University Press, 1970), 31.

5. Several paintings from the "Red Book" are reproduced in *Word and Image*, 66–73.

6. Letter of 29 June 1934 to G. A. Farner; in C. G. Jung, *Letters*, sel. and ed. Gerhard Adler and Aniela Jaffé, trans. R.F.C. Hull, Bollingen Series 95:1, vol. 1 (Princeton, NJ: Princeton University Press, 1973), 168.

7. Letter of 2 May 1925 to Henry A. Murray; *Letters*, 42.

8. "A Psychological Approach to the Dogma of the Trinity," in *Psychology and Religion: West and East*, trans. R.F.C. Hull (New York: Pantheon, 1958), 167.

9. Letter of 11 February 1956; cited in *Word and Image*, 196.

10. Letter of 5 January 1942 to Paul Schmitt; *Letters*, 309–10.

11. *Word and Image*, 188.

12. Jung's interpretations are provided in a letter of 13 December 1960; cited in *Word and Image*, 194.

13. In *The Archetypes and the Collective Unconscious*, trans. R.F.C. Hull, 2d ed. (Princeton, NJ: Princeton Univerity Press, 1968), 255–72; here 260.

14. Letter of 3 August 1953 to R.F.C. Hull; cited in *Word and Image*, 193.

15. Laurens von der Post, *Jung and the Story of Our Time* (New York: Random House/Vintage, 1977), 211.

Chapter Six
The Broken Towers

1. Letter of 8 June 1942; C. G. Jung, *Letters*, 318.

2. The political tendencies of all four writers (along with such modernists as T. S. Eliot and Ezra Pound) have been extensively studied. On Yeats see chap. 2, n. 39. In addition, see Edward A. Nickerson, "The Politics of Robinson Jeffers," in *Centennial Essays for Robinson Jeffers*, ed. Robert Zaller (Newark: University of Delaware Press, 1991), 254–67; Egon Schwarz, *Das verschluckte Schluchzen: Poesie und Politik bei Rainer Maria Rilke* (Frankfurt: Athenäum, 1972); J. P. Stern, *Hitler: The Führer and the People* (Glasgow: Fontana/Collins, 1975), 104–10; and Heinz Gess, *Von Faschismus zum Neuen Denken. C. G. Jungs Theorie im Wandel der Zeit* (Lüneburg: zu Klempen, 1994).

3. E.g., letter of 28 March 1934 to Max Guggenheim; C. G. Jung, *Letters*, 155–57.

4. Letter of 10 January 1939 to Bennett Cerf; *Selected Letters of Robinson Jeffers*, 271–72.

5. E.g., letters of September 1931 and February 1939; *Selected Letters of Robinson Jeffers*, 183 and 272.

6. Letter of 8 January 1948; C. G. Jung, *Letters*, 483.

7. James Olney, *The Rhizome and the Flower: The Perennial Philosophy— Yeats and Jung* (Berkeley and Los Angeles: University of California Press, 1980), 4–5.

8. See Timm, *W. B. Yeats*, 8 and 100.

9. T. S. Eliot, *The Complete Poems and Plays, 1909–1950* (New York: Harcourt, 1952), 48.

10. Pascal, *Pensées*, ed. Ch.-M. des Granges (Paris: Garnier, 1958), 90–91 (= art. 2, no. 72).

11. Sir James George Frazer, *The New Golden Bough*, new abridgment by Theodor H. Gaster (New York: New American Library/Mentor, 1964), xxvi.

12. This by now familiar story has been often rehearsed. See, for instance, Paul Johnson, *A History of the Modern World: From 1917 to the 1980s* (London: Weidenfeld and Nicolson, 1983), 1–48 ("A Relativistic World").

13. Thomas Mann, *Gesammelte Werke*, vol. 9 (Frankfurt am Main: Fischer, 1960), 58–173; here 165–66.

14. Virginia Woolf, "The Leaning Tower," in *The Moment and Other Essays* (New York: Harcourt/Harvest, 1974), 128–54; here 138.

15. Ibid., 139–40.

16. Virginia Woolf, *To the Lighthouse* (New York: Harcourt Brace Jovanovich/Harvest, n.d.), 276; the next passage, 301.

17. Malcolm Cowley, *Blue Juniata: Poems* (New York: Jonathan Cape & Harrison Smith, 1929), 73–74.

18. Eda Lou Walton, "Intolerable Towers," *English Journal* 19 (1930): 267–81, apparently adapts Cowley's phrase for the title of her perceptive article, which discusses the urban turn in American poetry of the 1920s. But she does not cite or discuss Cowley.

19. Hart Crane, *The Complete Poems and Selected Letters and Prose*, ed. Brom Weber (New York: Liveright, 1966), 217–23; here 218.

20. Ibid., 193–94.

21. Hofmannsthal defined his theory of "conservative revolution" most explicitly in his speech "Das Schrifttum als geistiger Raum der Nation" (1927), in *Prosa IV*, Gesammelte Werke in Einzelaufgaben, ed. Herbert Steiner (Frankfurt am Main: Fischer, 1955), 390–413.

22. For a comparison of Hofmannsthal's work with its source, see Egon Schwarz, *Hofmannsthal und Calderon*, Harvard Germanic Studies 3 (The Hague: Mouton, 1962), 91–112.

23. Both versions are reproduced in *Dramen IV*, Gesammelte Werke in Einzelausgaben, ed. Herbert Steiner (Frankfurt am Main: Fischer, 1958); here 360.

24. For differing interpretations of the versions, see William Rey, "Tragik und Verklärung des Geistes in Hofmannsthals *Der Turm*," *Euphorion* 47 (1953): 161–72; and Benjamin Bennett, *Hugo von Hofmannsthal: The Theaters of Consciousness* (Cambridge: Cambridge University Press, 1988), 326–41.

25. Hugo von Hofmannsthal, *Aufzeichnungen* (Frankfurt am Main: Fischer, 1959), 242.

26. On the tower as symbol of injustice as well as spiritual strength, see H. A. Hammelmann, *Hugo von Hofmannsthal* (New Haven: Yale University Press, 1957), 54–58.

27. Mathias Mayer, *Hugo von Hofmannsthal*, Sammlung Metzler 273 (Stuttgart: Metzler, 1993), 73–79.

28. Nigel Nicolson, "Focus on Country House Libraries: Sissinghurst," *Royal Oak Newsletter* (Summer 1996): 7.

29. Nigel Nicolson, *Portrait of a Marriage* (New York: Atheneum, 1973), 248.

30. V. Sackville-West, *Selected Poems* (London: Hogarth, 1941), 9.

31. V. Sackville-West, *Solitude: A Poem* (London: Hogarth, 1938), 7–8.

32. Harold Nicolson, *Diaries and Letters*, vol. 3 (New York: Atheneum, 1968), 262.

33. Claire Douglas, *Translate This Darkness: The Life of Christiana Morgan* (New York: Simon & Schuster, 1993), 223.

34. Ayn Rand, *The Fountainhead* (New York: New American Library/ Signet, 1971), 683. For a discussion of Rand's novel in an architectural context, see Andrew Saint, *The Image of the Architect* (New Haven: Yale University Press, 1983), 1–12.

35. Thomas Bernhard, *Die Erzählungen* (Frankfurt am Main: Suhrkamp, 1979), 7–79.

36. Jens Tismar, *Gestörte Idyllen* (Munich: Hanser, 1973), 112–19, mentions both Calderón and Hofmannsthal without developing the analogy.

37. Woody Allen, *Without Feathers* (New York: Random House, 1972), 117.

38. *Chronicle of Higher Education,* 25 March 1987.

INDEX

aere perennius (Horatian theme), 76, 93, 142, 181n.12
Aeschylus, *Oresteia*, 84
Allen, Woody, "The Irish Genius," 172
Anderson, Judith, 83
Andreas-Salomé, Lou, 100–101, 121–22
Apuleius, *The Golden Ass*, 15

Babel, Tower of, 11, 19, 29, 36–37, 62, 65; etymology of, 13
Babylon, tower of (Etemenanki), 10–13, 51, 65, 161, 168
Ballylee, Thoor. *See* Thoor Ballylee
Ballylee, village of, 46
Barbara, Saint, 16, 28, 34
Beardsley, Mabel, 43
Beckford, William, 25; *Vathek*, 25
Beebe, Maurice, 176n.34
Bender, Albert, 71
Berg, Alban, 156
Berkeley, George, 64
Bernhard, Thomas, *Amras*, 171–72
Bollingen, tower at, 5, 172. *See also* Jung, Carl Gustav
Bril, Paul, 19
Brophy, Robert J., 89
Browning, Robert, "Childe Roland to the Dark Tower Came," 31–32
Bruegel, Pieter, 19
Burke, Edmund, 25, 61, 64
Burton, Robert, *Anatomy of Melancholy*, 23

Calderón de la Barca, Pedro, *La vida es sueño*, 162–63
campaniles, 17
Campbell, Joseph, 6, 9
Carmel (Calif.), village of, 74
Carus, Carl Gustav, 26
Chartres, cathedral of, 104–5, 125
Château de Muzot. *See* Muzot
"conservative revolution," xi, 188n.21
cosmic mountain, 7, 37
Cowley, Malcolm, *Blue Juniata*, 159–60
Crane, Hart: "General Aims and Theories," 160; "The Broken Tower," 160–61

Danaë, 15, 28, 30, 34
Debussy, Claude, 157
de Chirico, Giorgio, 37
Delaunay, Robert, 37
Dinggedicht, 105
Donoghue, Denis, 180n.37
Droste-Hülshoff, Annette von, "At the Tower" ("Am Turme"), 27–28
Duino, Castle, 116, 123
Dumas, Alexandre, *La Tour des Nesle*, 26

Eiffel, Gustave, 34
Einstein, Albert, 156
Einsteinturm, 161
Eisner, Kurt, 116
Eliot, T. S., 112, 157; *The Waste Land*, 102, 154–55, 159
emblem books, 23

Engelberg, Edward, 180n.42
Etemenanki, 11, 174. *See also*
    Babylon, tower of
Euripides, Jeffers's adaptations of,
    83

Feininger, Lyonel, 37
Fonthill Abbey, 25
Frazer, Sir James, *The Golden Bough*,
    156
Freedman, Ralph, 184n.17
Freud, Sigmund, 11, 154, 156
Friedrich Caspar David, 26

Gide, André, *Paludes*, 35
Goethe, Johann Wolfgang von, 123,
    144–45, 147; *Faust*, 27, 73, 144–
    45; *Wilhelm Meister's Years of
    Apprenticeship*, 25
Goldsmith, Oliver, 64
Gonne, Maud, 43, 54
Gore-Booth, Constance (Countess
    Markievicz), 43–44
Grattan, Henry, 61
Gregory, Lady Augusta, 43, 45–46
Gregory, Robert, 43
gyres, Yeats's theory of, 62–63

Hardy, Thomas, *Two on a Tower*,
    33–34
Hauptmann, Gerhart, 5–6
Hawk Tower, 5, 71, 172; construction
    of, 79–80; name of, 80. *See also*
    Jeffers, Robinson
Heimann, Heidi, 184n.11
Herodotus, 10, 13
Hesse, Eva, 83
Hindemith, Paul, 6
Hitler, Adolf, 163
Hofmannsthal, Hugo von, 161, 163;
    The Tower (Der Turm), 161–65,
    171
Holbein, Hans, 19
Hölderlin, Friedrich, 123

Horace, 30, 95
Hugo, Hermann, *Pia Desideria*, 23
Hyde-Lees, Georgina (Mrs. W. B.
    Yeats), 46, 48

Ibsen, Henrik, *The Master Builder*, 36
"Inhumanism," 91, 95
Ivanov, V. I., 35
ivory tower, 29–31, 36, 38–39, 75

James, Henry, *The Ivory Tower*, 38–39
Jeffers, Robinson, 5–6, 133, 139,
    142–43, 151–54; building Tor
    House, 75–78; characteristics of his
    poetry, 76; constructing Hawk
    Tower, 79–80; education and mar-
    riage of, 72–74; and Lucretius,
    182n.33; his move to Carmel, 74–
    75; his obsession with stone, 77–78,
    83, 151; political views of, 82, 92–
    94; at Thoor Ballylee, 71, 181n.1;
    on Yeats, 81–82. Works: "Cassan-
    dra," 84; *Descent to the Dead*, 71;
    The Double Axe, 91, 152–53; early
    poems, 72; late poems, 93; "Mar-
    grave," 94–95, 151, 153; "Night
    without Sleep," 92; "The Old
    Stone-Mason," 77; "On Building
    with Stone," 77; "Poetry, Gongo-
    rism and a Thousand Years," 81–
    82; *Roan Stallion, Tamar and Other
    Poems*, 72; "Rock and Hawk," 78;
    Selected Poetry, 72; "Soliloquy," 94;
    "Star-Swirls," 93; *Tamar*, 72, 87;
    "To a Young Artist," 91; "To the
    Rock That Will Be a Cornerstone of
    the House," 77; "To the Stone-Cut-
    ters," 75; *The Tower beyond Trag-
    edy*, 83–91; "Watch the Lights
    Fade," 77
Jeffers, Una, 72–80, 153; her obses-
    sion with Ireland, 79
Joyce, James, *Ulysses*, 155
Jung, Dr. Carl, 144

Jung, Carl Gustav, 5–6, 151–54, 168; and building as image of psyche, 137–38; building tower-complex at Bollingen, 133, 135, 138–42; and early image of tower, 135–36; and Freud, 136–38; and Goethe, 144–45; lapidary mysticism of, 133–35, 151; and life at Bollingen, 146–48; and "Red Book," 139, 146; and stone emblems at Bollingen, 142–46

Kahler, Erich, *The Tower and the Abyss*, 155
Kaiser Wilhelm Memorial Church, 171
Kandinsky, Wassily, 156
Kanzog, Klaus, 185n.18
Kippenberg, Anton, 115, 122
Kircher, Athanasius, *Turris Babel*, 19
Klee, Paul, 156
Klossowska, Baladine (Merline), 116–21

Lander, Jeanette, 179n.27
Lane, Hugh, 44
Larsson, Hanna, 115
Lauretian litany, 30–31
Lechlitner, Ruth, 182n.35
Lewis, Sinclair, 74; *Elmer Gantry*, 174
Lucretian image of tower, 14, 27, 33, 36, 82, 95
Luther, Martin, 19–22, 39, 173
Lux, Joseph August, *Ingenieur-Ästhetik*, 36

MacLeish, Archibald, *Tower of Ivory*, 37–38
Maeterlinck, Maurice, *La Princesse Maleine*, 34, 50, 155, 162, 165
Mahler, Gustav, 157
Mann, Thomas, 157
Marguerite of Burgundy, 26

Markievicz, Countess, 43–44
Marx, Karl, 156
Mason, Lawrence, 38
Melville, Herman, "The Bell-Tower," 29
Mendelsohn, Erich, 161
Merline (Baladine Klossowska), 116–21
Milton, John, 26, 51–52, 54, 63, 81–82, 167; "Il Penseroso," 23
Minkowski, Helmut, 176n.21
"modernist," defined, xii–xiii
Montaigne, Michel de, 22–23, 33, 39, 167–68
Moore, Sturge, 62
Morgan, Christiana, 168
Moses, 11
mountains, 7, 11–12
Mulryne, J. R., 180n.43
Murray, Henry, 168
Mussolini, Benito, 153
Muzot, château de, 5, 117–23, 172

Nebuchadnezzar I, 11
Nebuchadnezzar II, 8, 11
Nietzsche, Friedrich, 32–33, 156
Norlind, Ernst, 115
nuraghi, 14, 144

O'Higgins, Kevin, 63
Oral Roberts University, 173–74
Orlik, Emil, 99

Palmer, Samuel, *The Lonely Tower*, 23
Panofsky, Erwin, 30
Pascal, Blaise, *Pensées*, 155–56
Philemon, 145, 152
Piranesi, Giambattista, 112
Poe, Edgar Allan, "The City in the Sea," 28–29, 36
political conservatism, 152–53
Pollexfen, Alfred, 43
Pound, Ezra, 49
pyramids, 7

Quinn, John, 55

Radcliffe, Ann, 25
Rafferty, Thomas, 47–48
Rand, Ayn, *The Fountainhead*, 168–71
Rapunzel, 15, 28
Rathenau, Walter, 128
Reicher, Hedwiga, 83–84
Reinhart, Werner, 118–19, 121, 127–29
Rilke, Rainer Maria, 5–6, 72, 133, 142, 151–54; in Belgium, 106–11; at Chartres, 104; at Muzot, 117–23, 127–30; and politics, 116, 128; in Russia, 101–3, 112; and Rodin, 103–6; and towers, 111–16. Works: *Book of Hours* (*Stundenbuch*), 102–3; *Duino Elegies* (*Duineser Elegien*), 116, 122–26, 129, 152, 154, 165–66; early poems, 99–101; "For Werner Reinhart," 128–29; "Furnes," 107–8, 110; "Die Kathedrale," 105–6; *Neue Gedichte*, 105; *The Notebooks of Malte Laurids Brigge*, 106, 113, 115; *Offerings to the Lares* (*Larenopfer*), 99; phallocentric poems, 114–15; "Quatrains Valaisans," 129; *Sonnets to Orpheus*, 122–23; "The Tower" ("Der Turm"), 108–11, 153; "Wendung," 113
Roberts, Reverend Oral, 173
Rodenbach, Georges, *Bruges-la-morte*, 107
Rodin, Auguste, 103–5, 113; *Tour du Travail*, 105
round towers, Irish, 17, 71, 79
Russell, Bertrand, 6

Sackville-West, Vita, 154–66; "Sissinghurst," 166–67; *Solitude*, 167
Sainte-Beuve, Charles-Augustin, "A M. Villemain," 30, 37

Les Saltimbanques (Picasso), 124
Sato, Junzo, 57, 65
Schinkel, Karl Friedrich, 26
Schönberg, Arnold, 157
Scott, William, 47–48
Serra, Father Junípero, 74–75
Shakespear, Olivia, 57
Shakespeare, William, 81
Shelley, Percy Bysshe, 25, 51–52, 54, 63–64, 81–82, 168; *Prince Athanase*, 26, 50; *Revolt of Islam*, 25–26
Simon the Stylite, 5
Sinclair, Upton, 74
Sissinghurst Castle, 165–66
skyscrapers, 37
Song of Songs, 30
Spengler, Oswald, 40
Stendhal, *La Chartreuse de Parme*, 27
Sterling, George, 87, 91
Stevenson, Robert Louis, *Treasure Island*, 74
Stravinsky, Igor, 157
Strawberry Hill, 25
Swift, Jonathan, 64
symbolists, French, 34–35, 51, 54, 63
Symons, Arthur, 46
Synge, John Millington, *Playboy of the Western World*, 44; *Riders to the Sea*, 79

templa serena, 14, 82. *See also* Lucretian image of tower
Tennyson, Alfred, 81
terrace temples, 8
thematics, defined, xiv
Thoor Ballylee, 5, 172; name of, 47. *See also* Yeats, William Butler
Thurn und Taxis, Princess Marie von, 116, 119, 122
Toller, Ernst, 116
Tolstoy, Leo, 112
Tornet, 35
Tour du Travail (Rodin), 105

tower: in antiquity, 13–16; as ascent of consciousness, 7, 62–63, 110–11, 152; in Christian Middle Ages, 17–18; as cosmic mountain, 6–7; defined, 6; in emblem books, 27; freestanding, 17; in Gothic romances, 25; as image of contemplation, 19–25; as locus of intellectual activity, 10; in medieval iconography, 23; as open symbol, 31–35; religious function of, 7–8; in Renaissance and Reformation, 19–23; in romanticism, 25–29; as seat of episcopal authority, 17; sexuality and sequestration in, 10–11; as skyscraper, 378; as symbol of civic authority, 17–18; symbolic associations with, 39; in French symbolism, 34–35. *See also* ivory tower; tower, lamp, and book
tower, lamp, and book (Miltonic image), 23, 25–26, 52–53, 56, 68, 167
"tower prohibition," 17
tribal towers, 19
Trickster, 146
Tuchman, Barbara, *The Proud Tower*, 36
Turmerlebnis, 19
turres ecclesiasticae, 17
turris eburnea, 30. *See also* ivory tower

Ullmann, Regine, 116

Valckenborch, Maerten van, 19
Van Doren, Mark, 78, 83, 91
Van Leeuwen, Thomas, "metaphysics of the skyscraper," 37
Veurne, town of, 107–11
Vigny, Alfred de, 30–31, 39
Villiers de l'Isle-Adam, Philippe-Auguste, *Axël*, 34–35, 50, 155, 162, 165
Virgil, *Eclogues*, 80

Walpole, Horace, 25
Walton, Eda Lou, 188n.18
Webern, Anton, 156
Westbrook, Edward Bruce, 179nn. 24 and 28, 180nn. 34 and 43
Westhoff, Clara, 104
Woolf, Virginia: "The Leaning Tower," 157–58, 165; *To the Lighthouse*, 158–59
Wordsworth, William, 81
Wunderly-Volkart, Nanny, 118–22

Yeats, William Butler, 5–6, 28, 72, 79, 81–82, 133, 142, 151–54, 168; his despair in 1919, 43–46; his early obsession with towers, 45–51; image of tower in his works, 51–55, 68; Jeffers on, 81–82; his move into Thoor Ballylee, 45–46; political views of, 43–45, 55, 63–64, 67–68; and restoration of Thoor Ballylee, 46–49. Works: "Among School Children," 59; "The Black Tower," 67–68; "Blood and the Moon," 51, 63–65; "Dialogue of Self and Soul," 65–67; "Ego Dominus Tuus," 52; *The Herne's Egg*, 51; "In Memory of Major Robert Gregory," 53, 62; "Lapis Lazuli," 51; "Meditations in Time of Civil War," 55–60, 62, 66; "Meru," 51; *Michael Robartes and the Dancer*, 43, 48; "Nineteen Hundred and Nineteen," 45; "Pages from a Diary," 68; "The Phases of the Moon," 52–53; "The Philosophy of Shelley's Poetry," 49–50; political poems of 1916, 43–44; "A Prayer for My Daughter," 54; "A Prayer on Going into My House," 53–54; *Rosa Alchemica*, 52; "Sailing to Byzantium," 59–61; "The Second Coming," 44, 152; "The Seven Sages," 64; "The Statues," 67; *Stories of Red Hanrahan*, 60;

Yeats, William Butler *(cont.)*
"Symbols," 65; "To Be Carved on a Stone at Thoor Ballylee," 48; "The Tower," 59–62, 151; *The Tower*, 55–56, 59, 62, 153; "The Trembling of the Veil," 52; *A Vision*, 63, 67, 154; *The Wanderings of Oisin*, 51; *The Wild Swans at Coole*, 43; *The Winding Stair*, 55, 62, 153.

ziggurat, 8–10, 160, 173; Hebrew view of, 11–13

ABOUT THE AUTHOR

Theodore Ziolkowski is Class of 1900 Professor
of German and Comparative Literature at
Princeton University. He has published nine
previous books with Princeton University Press,
including *German Romanticism and
Its Institutions, Virgil and the Moderns,*
and *The Mirror of Justice.*